200 stews & moroccan dishes

hamlyn | all color cookbook

200 stews &
moroccan dishes

Ghislaine Bénady and Nadjet Sefrioui

hamlyn

An Hachette UK Company
www.hachette.co.uk

First published in Great Britain in 2012 by
Hamlyn
a division of Octopus Publishing Group Ltd.,
Endeavour House, 189 Shaftesbury Avenue,
London, WC2H 8JY
www.octopusbooksusa.com

This edition published in 2013

Distributed in the USA by
Hachette Book Group USA
237 Park Avenue
New York, NY 10017 USA

Distributed in Canada by
Canadian Manda Group
165 Dufferin Street
Toronto, Ontario, Canada M6K 3H6

ISBN: 978-0-600-62509-4

Printed and bound in China

10 9 8 7 6 5 4 3 2 1

The U.S. Food and Drug Administration advises that eggs
should not be consumed raw. This book contains some
dishes made with raw or lightly cooked eggs. It is prudent for
vulnerable people, such as pregnant and nursing mothers,
people with weakened immune systems, the elderly, babies,
and young children, to avoid uncooked or lightly cooked
dishes made with eggs. Once prepared, these dishes should
be kept refrigerated and used promptly.

This book includes dishes made with nuts and nut derivatives.
It is advisable for those with known allergic reactions to
nuts and nut derivatives and those who may be potentially
vulnerable to these allergies to avoid dishes made with nuts and
nut oils. It is also prudent to check the labels of preprepared
ingredients for the possible inclusion of nut derivatives.

Standard kitchen spoon and cup measurements are used in all
recipes and are level unless otherwise indicated.

Ovens should be preheated to the specified temperature—if
using a convection oven, follow the manufacturer's
instructions for adjusting the time and temperature.

Fresh herbs should be used unless otherwise stated.

contents

introduction

In this book, the two authors share the delights and secrets of Moroccan cuisine through their own family recipes.

lemons, olives & argan oil

Preserved lemons and olives are indispensable ingredients in tagines, but they are just as essential as an hors d'oeuvre and can remain on the table as an accompaniment to the dishes that follow. In Morocco, preserved lemons are made with small, round fruit, but there is nothing to stop you from making them with larger, oval lemons (see page 18).

Delicatessens sell all kinds of marinated olives mixed with other ingredients, but you can also prepare them yourself: simply marinate chiles, garlic, cilantro, and roasted red pepper with the olives in a cool place for a day or two to impart their flavors.

Olive oil seasons vegetables and salads and its fruity aroma lifts and enhances the other ingredients, but argan oil adds a more delicate touch, a nutty aroma, to a whole range of salads, in particular, those using bell peppers. Tossing couscous grains in this oil gives them a wonderful flavor.

the cooking pot

The tagine, a Moroccan rustic dish, is a meat (or fish) stew that is slowly braised so the flavors mingle with not only the vegetables and spices but also with the dried fruits and preserved lemons (see page 18). The magic is performed by the lid of the traditional cooking utensil, a round, glazed terra-cotta dish that lends its name to the stew. Shaped like a tall conical chimney, it lets the trapped steam rise and fall, steaming the ingredients inside. It works on the principle of a braiser, effectively circulating the flavors and aromas. The tagine pot sits on a *braséro* or *kanoun*, which is also made in terra-cotta, but it can also be used on top of the stove with a heat-diffusing mat.

If you don't possess a tagine, a cast-iron pot or heavy casserole will do the job, because the secret of the dish also lies in cooking it long and slow over a low heat.

meat

Lamb, veal, chicken, duck, quail, and rabbit are the types of meat that work really well in a tagine. To be sure the meat becomes rich and melting, select your cuts carefully: too lean and you risk the meat drying out (this applies equally to meatballs). Using meat with a higher fat content means you don't have to add any extra to the dish.

For beef, center cut beef shanks or beef chuck are good choices; leg of veal likewise. Leg of lamb is the cut of choice, but shoulder is a less costly option. Ask your butcher to bone and trim the meat, then cut it into large pieces.

For poultry, use whole birds with plump, flavorsome meat, and either cut them yourself or ask the butcher to prepare them for you.

whole; later, they are quickly blanched and shelled. Spring to early summer is the season for fresh green beans, zucchini, eggplants, peas, and artichokes. Tomatoes, bell peppers, and cucumbers come into their own in summer and, by fall, it's time for turnips and quince. Cauliflower, celery, fennel, and pumpkin are the winter vegetables. The vegetables of the day typically determine the ingredients in a tagine, as with the choice of salads that precedes it.

vegetables

Onion, garlic, and fresh herbs are the pillars of Moroccan cuisine, but the choice of vegetables and fruit for a tagine should be determined by the season. In spring, the first tender fava beans are cooked

spices

The richness of Moroccan cuisine rests largely on the strongly aromatic flavors of the spices and spice mixes prepared by each cook. For example, ras-el-hanout is a mixture comprising up to thirty different

spices: saffron, cumin, coriander, ginger, turmeric, hot chili, paprika, cardamom, cinnamon, but also clove and star anise.

If you buy loose spices sold by weight, keep them in small quantities sealed in small jars so that they don't lose their flavor. Saffron, always used in minute quantities, is found in powdered form or in threads.

fish

The fish that are best suited to Moroccan cuisine are red snapper, sea bass, cod, pollock, tuna, porgy (which are also called scup or sea bream), whiting, hake, and swordfish—as well as the indispensable sardine, the bounty of the Moroccan seas, which is at its best when simply served broiled or grilled. All these fish can be baked in the oven, fried, stuffed, made into fish balls, or simmered in a tagine with vegetables.

couscous & chickpeas

It is certainly tempting to use precooked couscous in a couscous dish. However, while it's true that there are good-quality versions around and that they will save you time, the traditional method is also part of the pleasure of Moroccan cuisine, and mastering it is not as complicated as it seems. If available, use medium-grain, dry couscous. As for chickpeas, don't hesitate to forego the soaking stage and buy without guilt a good-quality brand of prepared canned beans.

dried fruit

The use of dried fruit in Moroccan cuisine, which give many recipes their sweet–sour flavor and unique character, is a Persian influence, introduced by the Arabs. Dates, figs, and prunes find their way into these dishes and their flesh thickens sauces and flavors the meat.

bread

To a Moroccan, bread (*khobz* or, in rural areas, *kesra*) is sacred and must never be squandered. All that is required is some flour (white or whole-wheat), a little water, sugar, and salt, a little yeast, and a light working (the dough must not rise too much); then the loaves rest wrapped in cloth before being placed on a large baking sheet. The bread is shaped into flat circles and has only one rising. Anise seeds or sesame seeds are often worked into the dough or sprinkled on the light crust. The soft interior is fairly light to absorb the sauce of a tagine, but it must also be sufficiently dense to carry other food to the mouth—in Morocco food is traditionally eaten without cutlery. Food is eaten with the thumb, index finger, and middle finger of one hand, with the aid of a piece of bread. Flatter loaves serve to sandwich kebab meat.

fruits

In all Moroccan homes, meals end with fresh fruit. During celebratory meals, beautifully arranged fruit—either piled

on platters or sometimes on a bed of ice—is served in praise and celebration of the season. If the fruit is prepared, it is scented with orange-flower water, dusted with cinnamon, or strewn with crushed nuts. Indeed, nothing is more refreshing at the end of a meal than a simple salad of oranges or a pomegranate with a sprinkling of orange-flower water and a light dusting of confectioners' sugar. Shredded carrot can also be served in the same way.

pastries

Moroccans end a meal more often with fruit than a sweet pastry. And although traditional desserts are fairly unusual, something sweet between courses—milk rice pudding, for example—is extremely popular. Moroccan pastries are similar to those of the Middle East, albeit different in appearance. Almonds reign supreme, especially finely ground. Confectioners' sugar, cinnamon, orange-flower water, rose water, and honey are popular. Nuts, dates, dried figs, sesame seeds, and, to a lesser degree, pistachio nuts play a role in the art of the pastry chef. And if these delicious morsels rarely round off a meal, they are the preferred accompaniment to mint tea, the ubiquitous drink in Morocco, offered as a gesture of welcome.

how to make couscous

3 cups **medium-grain couscous**

1 tablespoon **salt**

1 tablespoon **sunflower oil**

2 cups cold **water**

3 tablespoons **butter,** softened

Put the couscous in a wide, shallow dish or baking pan so that it can be spread out.

Add the salt and pour the oil over the couscous, stirring it in with a fork to keep the grains separate.

Gradually sprinkle with the water. Let the couscous grains swell for 5 minutes, then coat your hands with sunflower oil and work through the couscous, lifting and aerating it.

Let the couscous rest for 10 minutes, aerating it occasionally with your fingers so that it doesn't stick.

Put the couscous in the upper section of a couscous steamer and place above boiling stock. Check that the two sections of the steamer fit tightly together to make sure that the steam doesn't escape.

Make little holes in the couscous with the tip of a wooden spoon.

As soon as the steam starts to escape, transfer the couscous to the wide, shallow bowl. Sprinkle with a glass of water and aerate again, this time with a wooden spoon to avoid burning yourself.

Return the couscous to the upper section of the couscous steamer and repeat the cooking instructions in steps 6–7, then add the softened butter. Aerate the couscous with your hands again, incorporating the butter.

Again let it rest for a few moments, then separate the grains, mixing the couscous with both hands to distribute the butter thoroughly.

how to make pastilla

Butter a round baking pan or pie plate.

Lay 2 sheets of oiled and buttered phyllo pastry on top.

Coat your fingers with a light mixture of flour and water, stick 4 more sheets of pastry around the rim, leaving most of each sheet draped off the pan in the way that petals are arranged around the center of a flower.

Lay another phyllo sheet on the baking pan and butter well.

Spread a layer of filling over the bottom of the pastry.

Arrange the other ingredients evenly.

Cover with another sheet of pastry.

Fold in the "petals," sticking each one to the others with the flour-and-water mix.

Finish with a final sheet of pastry, sticking it around the edges. Butter the surface well.

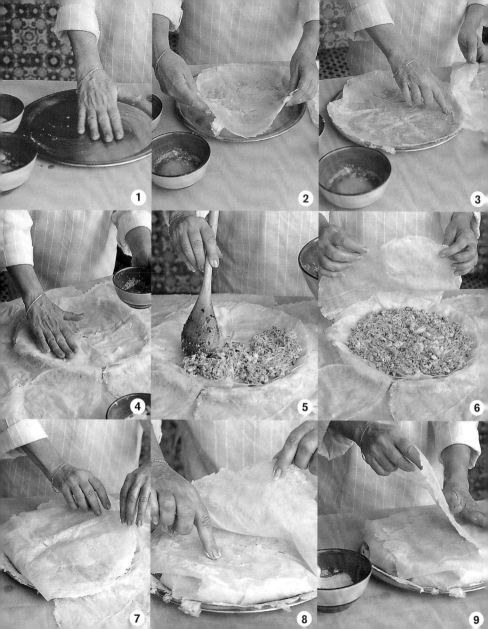

kemia &
small first
courses

preserved lemons

Makes **10**
Soaking time **1 day**
Maceration time **3 weeks**

10 **unwaxed lemons**
   (about 2 lb)
1 cup **kosher salt**

Wash the lemons thoroughly before soaking them in cold water for a day, changing the water two or three times.

Make two fairly deep incisions in the form of a cross in each lemon, starting at the tip. Open the cut as much as possible and fill with salt.

Arrange the filled lemons immediately in one or more mason jars, packing them tightly and firming them down—it should be difficult to close the lid.

Let macerate for 3 weeks.

For marinated black olives, mix 1 cup extra-virgin olive oil with 6 finely chopped garlic cloves, 2 lemons cut into chunks, 12 black peppercorns, ¼ cup of thyme leaves, and 1 teaspoon of oregano leaves in a mason jar. Add 2¼ cups ripe black olives. Let marinate for at least a day.

shrimp cigars

Makes **40**

Preparation time **20 minutes**

Cooking time **25 minutes**

1 tablespoon **sunflower oil**

1 lb cooked, peeled **shrimp**, deveined

2 **garlic cloves**, crushed

1 large bunch of **flat-leaf parsley**, chopped

1 large bunch of **cilantro**, chopped

½ tablespoon **sweet paprika**

¼ teaspoon **cayenne pepper**

2 **eggs**, beaten

egg white, for sealing

10 sheets **phyllo pastry**

oil for frying

salt

Heat the oil in a large skillet and cook the shrimp, garlic, and herbs. Season with the spices and cook until the mixture comes away from the skillet. Add the eggs and quickly mix in. Remove from the heat and let cool.

Meanwhile, separate the phyllo sheets. Cut each into four squares and fold each square into a triangle. Place some of the filling along the longest edge of each triangle, almost to the ends. Tuck in the ends over the filling, then roll up the cigar toward the point. Seal the pastry with a dab of egg white.

Heat the oil until a cube of bread browns in 30 seconds and deep-fry the cigars, in batches, until golden. Drain on paper towels before serving.

For meat cigars, first prepare the filling. Soften a finely chopped medium onion in 1 tablespoon of sunflower oil, then add 1 lb ground beef or lamb, 1 teaspoon of ground cinnamon, and ¼ teaspoon of ground ginger. Season to taste with salt and black pepper and cook, stirring, for 10 minutes, or until the meat browns. Stir in 2 tablespoons each of cilantro and flat-leaf parsley. Add 3 lightly beaten eggs and quickly mix in. Remove from the heat and let cool. Complete the recipe as above.

fried pastries with goat cheese

Makes **20**
Preparation time **30 minutes**
Cooking time **5 minutes**

8 oz fresh **goat cheese**
1/2 teaspoon **thyme leaves**
10 **Greek black olives**, pitted
and coarsely chopped
1 **egg**, beaten
5 sheets **phyllo pastry**
egg white, for sealing
oil, for frying
salt and **black pepper**

Mix together the goat cheese with the thyme and the olives in a salad bowl. Season with salt and black pepper and bind with the egg. Set aside.

Separate the phyllo pastry sheets. Brush each one with the oil, then cut into 4 strips.

Take the pastry strips one at a time and place 1/2 teaspoon of filling about 1 inch from the nearest end. Fold the pastry over and over to wrap the filling in a triangle, then seal the end with a little egg white. Repeat with all the strips.

Heat the oil until a cube of bread browns in 30 seconds and deep-fry the pastries, in batches, until golden on both sides. Drain on paper towels.

Serve hot, with lettuce leaves, if you desire.

For baked pastries with goat cheese, prepare the filling as above, replacing the thyme leaves with 4 cups lightly steamed fresh spinach, well drained and finely chopped. Melt 6 tablespoons butter and set aside. Use 10 sheets of phyllo, cutting each one in half lengthwise. Prepare the pastries as above, folding each pastry strip in half lengthwise and brushing with the melted butter before adding the filling and folding into triangles. Place the pastries on a greased baking sheet, brush with the remaining melted butter, then bake in a preheated oven, at 350°F, for 30 minutes, until crisp and golden.

...hing salad

Ser...
Preparation time **15 minutes**

2 **tomatoes**
1 small **cucumber**
1 small **green bell pepper**
2 **scallions**
1 small **chile** (optional)
2 quarters of **preserved
   lemon**, rind only
1 tablespoon **vinegar**
2 tablespoons **olive oil**
½ teaspoon **ground cumin**
½ teaspoon **mild paprika**
salt and **black pepper**
whole **ripe black olives**,
   to garnish

Peel the tomatoes and cucumber and remove the seeds from the tomatoes and the bell pepper.

Cut all the vegetables and the lemon rind into small dice and place in a salad bowl.

Dress with the vinegar, oil, spices, and salt and black pepper and garnish with a few black olives.

For cucumber and mint salad, peel a large cucumber and grate it into a strainer placed over a bowl. Set aside for 15 minutes to let the juices drain. Mix with 3 tablespoons of olive oil, 1 tablespoon of finely chopped preserved lemon, and 2 tablespoons of chopped mint leaves. Season to taste with black pepper.

fekkas

Serves **8–10**
Preparation time **15 minutes**,
plus resting
Cooking time **25 minutes**

2¼ teaspoons (1 envelope)
  active dry yeast
8 cups **all-purpose flour**
½ teaspoon **cayenne pepper**
½ teaspoon **salt**
2 cups shredded **Gruyère
  cheese** or **Swiss cheese**
⅔ cup **peanut oil**
2 tablespoons **butter**, melted

Put all the ingredients into a large bowl and mix well. Work with your hands, adding a little lukewarm water, if necessary, until you have a soft, pliable dough.

Form the dough into rolls the size of a fat cigar and place on a greased baking sheet. Bake for 15 minutes without browning. Let rest for 24 hours.

Cut the rolls into slices ¼ inch thick and arrange on a baking sheet. Place in a preheated oven, at 350°F, and brown for 3 minutes.

For harissa fekkas, replace the Gruyère cheese with the same quantity of extra-sharp cheddar cheese. Omit the cayenne pepper and reduce the quantity of peanut oil to ½ cup. Stir 2 tablespoons of harissa (see page 76) into the oil before adding it to the mixture.

almond bites

Serves **6–8**

Preparation time **20 minutes**

Cooking time **15 minutes**

1¾ cups **whole almonds**

2 sheets **ready-to-bake puff pastry**

1 **egg yolk**, beaten, to glaze

Sprinkle the almonds with salted water and toast for about 10 minutes in a skillet over medium heat, stirring from time to time.

Preheat the oven to 400°F.

Remove the pastry from the refrigerator, roll out, and cut into circles, using a 1½ inch pastry cutter. Place an almond in the center of each, fold over to enclose, and glaze with the egg yolk.

Place on a greased baking sheet and cook for 15 minutes.

For spicy almond bites, gently toast 1 teaspoon each of caraway, coriander, and cumin seeds in a small saucepan. Using a mortar and pestle, grind the spices with 1 teaspoon each of dried red pepper flakes and sea salt and ½ teaspoon of black pepper. Stir in 1 tablespoon of Demerara sugar. Gently sauté the almonds in 2 tablespoons of sunflower oil, stirring frequently, until pale golden, then stir in the spice mix and cook for another 4–5 minutes to coat the almonds. Complete the recipe as above.

beef & gruyère pastries

Makes **12**
Preparation time **30 minutes**
Cooking time **25 minutes**

3 **eggs**
2 tablespoons **butter**
8 oz **ground beef**
1 bunch of **flat-leaf parsley**, snipped
pinch of **saffron**
1 cup shredded **Gruyère cheese**,
2 sheets **ready-to-bake puff pastry**
salt and **black pepper**

Hard boil 1 egg, then cool under cold running water.

Meanwhile, melt the butter in a skillet with the salt and black pepper and brown the beef for 5 minutes. Let cool.

Peel the hard-boiled egg and chop it finely into a salad bowl. Add the parsley, saffron, beef, cheese, and 1 raw egg. Mix together by hand.

Preheat the oven to 350°F.

Roll out the pastry and cut into 12 small circles with a pastry cutter or using a glass. Place a little of the filling in the center of each, fold over to enclose, and brush each one with the third egg, beaten, to glaze and seal.

Place on a greased baking sheet and bake for 15 minutes.

For lamb & feta pastries, melt 2 tablespoons butter in a skillet and add 1 finely chopped small onion and 2 tablespoons of pine nuts. Cook over medium heat, stirring constantly, for 4–5 minutes, to color the pine nuts, then stir in 1 teaspoon of ras-el-hanout. Add 8 oz ground lamb and cook, stirring constantly, for 5 minutes to brown the meat. Let cool, then stir in ⅔ cup crumbled feta cheese and a little salt and black pepper. Complete the recipe as above.

savory anise cookies

Serves **6–8**
Preparation time **10 minutes**,
    plus resting
Cooking time **10 minutes**

2¹⁄₃ cups **all-purpose flour**
²⁄₃ cup **cornstarch**
2 **eggs**, beaten
1 cup shredded **Gruyère
    cheese** or **Swiss cheese**
1¾ sticks **butter**, softened
2 tablespoons **milk**
1 teaspoon **baking powder**
¼ teaspoon **salt**
¼ teaspoon **black pepper**
¼ teaspoon **ground anise
    seeds**
½ teaspoon **sesame seeds**
1 **egg yolk**, beaten, to glaze

Mix the flour and cornstarch with the eggs, then add all the remaining ingredients except the beaten egg yolk. Work rapidly with your hands without overkneading, then let the dough rest in the refrigerator for 1 hour.

Preheat the oven to 400°F.

Remove the dough and roll out. Cut out the cookies with a 1 inch pastry cutter. Place on a greased baking sheet and glaze the tops with the egg yolk. Bake for 10 minutes.

For anise seed bread, place 2¼ cups all-purpose flour in a mixing bowl and stir in 2¼ teaspoons (1 envelope) of active dry yeast and 2 teaspoons each of whole anise seeds and salt. Stir in 1 tablespoon of olive oil and 1¹⁄₃ cups warm water, then gradually add about 2¼ cups all-purpose flour to make a dough. Knead for 10 minutes until smooth, then place in an oiled bowl, cover, and set aside for 1½ hours, or until doubled in size. Punch out the air, then divide the dough into two balls, place on a greased baking sheet, flatten into circles, cover, and set aside for 20 minutes. Prick the sides with a fork, then brush the tops with egg white whisked with 1 teaspoon of water and sprinkle each with 1 tablespoon of sesame seeds. Cook in a preheated oven, at 375°F, for about 30 minutes, until golden.

beet & cumin salad

Serves **6**
Preparation time **5 minutes**

3 medium **beets**, cooked
1 **garlic clove**, crushed
½ teaspoon **ground cumin**
1 **lemon**, juiced
1 tablespoon **olive oil**
salt

Peel the beets, cut it into small pieces, and place in a small bowl with the garlic.

Season to taste with salt and the cumin.

Drizzle the lemon juice and oil over the beets. Mix together and serve chilled.

For carrot & cumin salad, trim and peel 10 carrots (about 1¼ lb) . Cut them into large batons and steam for 10–15 minutes, until just tender. Heat ¼ cup of olive oil in a skillet and sauté the carrots with 4 crushed garlic cloves, 1 teaspoon of ground cumin, and ½ teaspoon of paprika until the garlic begins to brown. Season to taste with salt and black pepper and serve drizzled with 1 tablespoon of lemon juice.

eggplant "caviar"

Serves **6**

Preparation time **15 minutes**

Cooking time **15 minutes**

2 **eggplants** (about 2 lb)

4 **tomatoes** (about 2 lb)

½ teaspoon **ground cumin**

½ teaspoon **paprika**

½ bunch of **cilantro**, snipped

½ bunch of **flat-leaf parsley**, snipped

3 **garlic cloves**, crushed

⅔ cup **water**

2 tablespoons **olive oil**

salt

preserved lemon and **lemon-marinated olives**, to garnish

Trim and partly peel the eggplants, leaving strips of the skin intact, then dice the flesh.

Peel the tomatoes, squeeze them to release the juice, then dice the flesh.

Place the eggplants and tomatoes with the spices in a pressure cooker and add the herbs and the garlic. Add the water and oil, and season with salt. Mix well, close the lid firmly, cook over gentle heat for 10 minutes, then remove the lid and let the "caviar" reduce. If you do not have a pressure cooker, place the ingredients in a heavy flameproof casserole or saucepan as above, cover, and cook over gentle heat for 30 minutes. Remove the lid and let the "caviar" reduce before serving.

Serve garnished with strips of preserved lemon and lemon-marinated olives.

For roasted eggplant & tomato salad, prick 1 large eggplant all over with a sharp knife, then roast in a preheated oven, at 475°F, for about 45 minutes, until soft. Cool then peel. Drain, chop, and mash the eggplant well in a colander to release the juices. Over low heat, reduce 4 peeled and chopped tomatoes to a thick sauce with 4 chopped garlic cloves and a pinch of salt. Stir in the eggplant, the juice of 1 lemon, ¼ cup of olive oil, 1 teaspoon of ground cumin, ½ teaspoon of paprika, and 2 tablespoons each of chopped cilantro and flat-leaf parsley. Season to taste and serve garnished as above.

chicken & hummus wraps

Serves **4**
Preparation time **5 minutes**
Cooking time **10 minutes**

6 skinless **chicken thighs**
(about 1 lb in total)
2 tablespoons **extra-virgin olive oil**
grated rind and juice of
1 **lemon**
1 **garlic clove**, crushed
1 teaspoon **ground cumin**
4 **flour tortillas**
¾ cup **hummus**
1 large handful **arugula leaves**
1 handful **parsley leaves**
salt and **black pepper**

Cut the chicken thighs into quarters and put in a bowl. Combine the oil, lemon rind, garlic, and cumin, season with salt and black pepper, add to the chicken, and stir well.

Heat a ridged grill pan until hot. Thread the chicken pieces onto metal skewers, add to the pan, and cook for 4–5 minutes on each side. Remove and let rest for 5 minutes.

Meanwhile, warm the tortillas in a preheated oven, at 350°F, for 5 minutes.

Remove the chicken from the skewers. Divide the hummus, arugula, parsley, and chicken among the tortillas. Squeeze the lemon juice over the filling, wrap, and serve.

For easy homemade hummus, put 1 (15 oz) can drained chickpeas, 1 crushed garlic clove, 3 tablespoons of extra-virgin olive oil, 1 tablespoon of lemon juice, and salt and black pepper to taste in a food processor or blender and process until smooth.

moroccan carrot salad

Serves **4–6**
Preparation time **10 minutes**
Cooking time **15–20 minutes**

2 bunches of **carrots**, trimmed
spray oil
3 tablespoons **sunflower
    seeds**, toasted
2 tablespoons chopped
    parsley

Dressing
¼ cup **extra-virgin olive oil**
2 tablespoons **white wine
    vinegar**
1 **garlic clove**, finely chopped
1 teaspoon **pomegranate
    syrup**
1 teaspoon **honey**
salt and **black pepper**

Blanch the carrots in a large saucepan of lightly salted boiling water for 10 minutes. Drain well and pat dry.

Transfer to a bowl and spray with a little oil, then cook on a hot barbecue for 5–10 minutes, turning frequently, until charred.

Meanwhile, combine the dressing ingredients in a large bowl and season to taste. Stir in the cooked carrots, sunflower seeds, and parsley and toss well. Serve hot.

For spiced carrot salad, mix 4 cups peeled and shredded carrots with the chopped flesh of 2 oranges. Make a dressing from 2 tablespoons of orange juice, 1 tablespoon of lemon juice, 2 tablespoons of olive oil, 1 teaspoon of sugar, and ½ teaspoon each of ground cumin and cinnamon. Season with salt and black pepper. Toss the carrot and orange mixture in the dressing, then stir in a handful of chopped cilantro. Garnish with cilantro sprigs to serve.

roasted peppers with argan oil

Serves **6**
Preparation time **5 minutes**
Cooking time **20 minutes**

6 large **red bell peppers**
3 **garlic cloves**, cut into
   tiny pieces
1 **lemon**, juiced
½ teaspoon **ground cumin**
2 tablespoons **argan oil**
salt

Preheat the broiler and roast the bell peppers, turning occasionally, until the skin starts to blacken on all sides.

Remove from the heat and put in a plastic bag to cool. Once cool, remove the skins and seed. Cut the flesh into pieces.

Put the roasted peppers in a bowl and mix with the garlic, lemon juice, cumin, oil, and salt to taste. Serve cold.

For roasted pepper & chickpea salad, prepare 4 large red bell peppers as above. Mix a 15 oz can of chickpeas, rinsed and drained, with 2 crushed garlic cloves, the juice of 1 lemon, and 3 tablespoons of olive oil. Add 1 teaspoon of chopped oregano, season with salt and black pepper, and mix well. Gently fold in the roasted peppers.

roasted peppers with lemon

Serves **6**
Preparation time **5 minutes**
Cooking time **20 minutes**

6 large **green bell peppers**
3 **garlic cloves**, cut into tiny
   pieces
1 **lemon**, juiced
½ teaspoon **ground cumin**
2 tablespoons **olive oil**
salt

Preheat the broiler and roast the bell peppers, turning occasionally, until the skin starts to blacken on all sides.

Remove from the heat and put in a plastic bag to cool. Once cool, remove the skins and seed. Cut the flesh into pieces.

Put the roasted peppers in a bowl and mix with the garlic, lemon juice, cumin, oil, and salt to taste. Serve cold.

For roasted red pepper dip, prepare 6 red bell peppers as above. Blend the chopped roasted peppers to a puree in a food processor with 2 crushed garlic cloves, the juice of 1½ lemons, 1 teaspoon of ground cumin, a pinch of chili powder, ¼ cup of olive oil, and salt to taste. To serve, stir 2 tablespoons each of chopped cilantro and flat-leaf parsley into the dip with the chopped peel of ½ a preserved lemon.

roasted pepper & tomato salad

Serves **6**
Preparation time **10 minutes**
Cooking time **20 minutes**

4 **green bell peppers**
½ **preserved lemon**
8 **tomatoes** (about 2 lb)
3 tablespoons **olive oil**
salt

Preheat the broiler and roast the bell peppers, turning occasionally, until the skin starts to blacken on all sides.

Remove from the heat and put in a plastic bag to cool. Once cool, remove the skins and seed.

Meanwhile, soak the preserved lemon in warm water for 5 minutes to remove the salt.

Peel the tomatoes, remove the seeds and juice, and cut the flesh into slices.

Cut the roasted peppers into long slices and add the tomatoes and the preserved lemon, cut into tiny pieces. Dress with the oil and salt to taste.

For tomatoes stuffed with roasted peppers, prepare 4 red bell peppers as above and cut them into fine strips. Mix with ¼ cup of chopped ripe black olives, 1 tablespoon of toasted pine nuts, the chopped peel of ½ a preserved lemon, and 2 tablespoons each of capers and chopped flat-leaf parsley. Cut the tops off 6 large tomatoes, then scoop out the centers and seeds with a teaspoon. Fill with the roasted pepper mixture, replace the tops and bake in an oiled ovenproof dish in a preheated oven, at 350°F, for about 20 minutes, until softened.

crispy lamb moroccan rolls

Serves **2**
Preparation time **15 minutes**
Cooking time **10 minutes**

8 oz **ground lamb**
1 teaspoon **ground cinnamon**
3 tablespoons **pine nuts**
2 **naans**, warmed
¾ cup **hummus**
2 tablespoons **mint leaves**
1 **Boston lettuce**, finely
    shredded (optional)

Sauté the ground lamb in a large, nonstick skillet for 8–10 minutes, until it becomes golden brown. Add the cinnamon and pine nuts and cook again for 1 minute. Remove from the heat.

Place the warmed naans on a cutting board and, using a rolling pin, firmly roll to flatten.

Mix the hummus with half the mint leaves, then spread in a thick layer over the warmed naans. Spoon the crispy lamb over the hummus, then sprinkle with the shredded lettuce, if using, and the remaining mint leaves. Tightly roll up and secure with toothpicks.

Serve immediately.

For lamb kofta, mix the raw ground lamb with 4 finely chopped scallions, 1 teaspoon of ground cinnamon, a finely chopped tomato, and 1 egg yolk until blended together. Form into a large, thin patty shape and broil or cook in a large, heavy skillet on one side for 3 minutes, then on the other side for 2 minutes, until golden. Spread 1 warm naan with 2 tablespoons of Greek yogurt, sprinkle with the mint leaves and shredded lettuce, if using, and slip the large flattened kofta on top. Roll tightly and secure with toothpicks. Cut the kofta in half to serve 2.

sweet potato & raisin salad

Serves **6**
Preparation time **15 minutes**
Cooking time **25 minutes**

6 **sweet potatoes** (about 2 lb)
²/₃ cup **raisins**
1 tablespoon **peanut oil**
4 tablespoons **butter**
1 small **onion**, peeled and
   finely grated
½ teaspoon **ground ginger**
pinch of **saffron threads**
1 cup **water**
½ teaspoon **ground cinnamon**
1 tablespoon **sugar**
1 tablespoon **honey**
pinch of **salt** and **black pepper**

Peel the sweet potatoes and cut into 1 inch thick slices or pieces.

Soak the raisins in a bowl of hot water for 5 minutes.

Heat the oil and butter in a large, heavy flameproof casserole and soften the onion over gentle heat. Add the spices, salt, and black pepper and stir for 5 minutes. Moisten with the water. Once it bubbles, add the sweet potatoes and cook for 10 minutes.

Add the drained raisins, then the cinnamon, sugar, and honey. Lower the heat and let simmer for 10 minutes, until the sauce is thick and rich.

Serve warm.

For spicy sweet potato salad, sauté 2 chopped onions in 3 tablespoons of olive oil until golden. Add 1 teaspoon each of ground ginger, ground cumin, and paprika, plus a pinch of salt, and stir for 5 minutes, then add the water and sweet potatoes as above. To serve, stir in the juice of 1 lemon, the chopped peel of a preserved lemon, and 12 green olives. Drizzle with extra olive oil and garnish with finely chopped flat-leaf parsley.

orange & olive salad

Serves **6**
Preparation time **15 minutes**
Refrigeration **1 hour**

3 large **oranges**
3 **garlic cloves**, finely chopped
½ teaspoon **chili powder**
2 tablespoons **olive oil**
2 tablespoons **lemon juice**
(about 1 lemon)
1½ cups **Greek ripe
black olives**
salt

Peel the oranges, removing all pith and membrane. Cut the segments into pieces and put into a salad bowl.

Add the garlic to the bowl.

Season with the chili powder, oil, lemon juice, and salt to taste. Gently incorporate the olives.

Chill in the refrigerator for at least 1 hour. Serve cold.

For orange, olive & onion salad, prepare the oranges as above and sprinkle with the olives and a finely chopped mild red onion. Sprinkle with a dressing made with the juice of 1 lemon, 2 tablespoons of olive oil, ¼ teaspoon each of ground cumin and paprika, a pinch of chili powder, and salt to taste. Garnish with finely chopped flat-leaf parsley to serve.

garlic-fried chiles

Serves **6**
Preparation time **15 minutes**
Cooking time **5 minutes**

oil, for frying
6 **green chiles**
2 **garlic cloves**, crushed
salt

Heat a little oil in a skillet and sauté the chiles, turning regularly. Transfer to a plate covered with paper towels, then arrange in a shallow dish.

Brown the garlic rapidly in the skillet.

Season the chiles with the garlic and salt to taste.

For garlic-roasted tomatoes, cut 12 ripe plum tomatoes in half lengthwise and place, cut side up, in an ovenproof dish brushed with 2 tablespoons of olive oil. Tuck the unpeeled cloves from a whole head of garlic between the tomatoes. Sprinkle with 2 tablespoons of sugar, season with salt and black pepper to taste, and roast for 4 hours in a preheated oven, at 275°F.

tapenade

Serves **6**
Preparation time **15 minutes**

3 cups **Greek ripe
black olives**
2 **garlic cloves**, crushed
1 tablespoon **thyme** or
marjoram
2 tablespoons **olive oil**
pinch of **salt**

Pit the olives and place in a salad bowl.

Mix the garlic with the olives.

Add the herbs, oil, and salt and mix well.

Serve well chilled.

For green olive tapenade, finely chop together 3 cups
pitted green olives, 1 tablespoon of capers, and 1 (2 oz)
can anchovies. Stir in 2 tablespoons of olive oil, the juice
of 1 lemon, 2 tablespoons of finely chopped flat-leaf
parsley, and 2 crushed garlic cloves. Mix well.

soups

harira fassia

Serves **6**
Preparation time **15 minutes**
Cooking time **40 minutes**

4 ripe **tomatoes**
1 tablespoon **tomato paste**
2½ cups **water**
⅓ cup **all-purpose flour**
2 cups **butter**
2 **onions**, finely chopped
8 oz **veal**, cubed
4 oz **lamb**, cubed
1 cup drained **canned chickpeas**
a few **celery leaves**
2 bunches of **cilantro**, chopped
1 bunch of **flat-leaf parsley**, chopped
¼ teaspoon **black pepper**
1 envelope of **saffron colorant**
pinch of **powdered saffron**
¼ teaspoon **ground ginger**
½ cup **green lentils**
¼ cup **short-grain rice**
salt

Peel the tomatoes and cut into small pieces.

Blend the tomato paste with the half the water and the flour.

Place the butter in a large, heavy flameproof casserole with the tomatoes, onions, veal, lamb, chickpeas, celery leaves, half the cilantro, all the parsley, spices, and salt to taste. Cover with water and cook for 15 minutes, then add the lentils.

Let cook for another 10 minutes, until everything is cooked through, then add the remaining measured water. As soon as it returns to a boil, add the diluted tomato paste and stir with a spatula for 10 minutes to prevent lumps from forming.

Add the rice 15 minutes before the end.

Serve sprinkled with the remaining cilantro.

For harira with pasta, omit the rice and add 3 oz orzo or crushed vermicelli with the juice of 1 lemon about 10 minutes before serving the soup. Garnish with lemon wedges and the remaining cilantro and accompany with fresh dates.

couscous & anise soup

Serves **6**
Preparation time **2 minutes**
Cooking time **18 minutes**

6 cups **water**
4 tablespoons **butter**
½ teaspoon **ground turmeric**
¼ teaspoon **black pepper**
1 cup **coarse-grain couscous**
1 tablespoon **ground
  anise seeds**
salt

Put the water, butter, turmeric, black pepper, and salt to taste in a large saucepan. Bring to a boil, then add the couscous in a steady stream with half the anise seeds.

Let simmer for 15 minutes over low heat, stirring from time to time during cooking to prevent lumps from forming. If the couscous swells too much, add a little extra water.

Stir in the remaining anise seeds and serve hot.

For chicken and couscous soup, sauté a chopped onion in 2 tablespoons of olive oil until translucent. Add 1 lb skinless, boneless chicken breast, cut into strips, and cook, stirring, for 2 minutes. Add a medium sweet potato and a medium zucchini, cut into cubes, the couscous, half the anise seeds, and the water. Simmer for 15 minutes over low heat, as above. Stir in the remaining anise seeds and serve hot, sprinkled with 1 tablespoon of chopped flat-leaf parsley.

harira

Serves **8–10**
Preparation time **about
25 minutes**, plus soaking
Cooking time **about 3 hours**

1 ⅓ cups **dried chickpeas**,
soaked in cold water
overnight
2 **chicken breasts**, halved
5 cups **chicken stock**
5 cups **water**
1 (28 oz) can **diced tomatoes**
¼ teaspoon crumbled **saffron
threads** (optional)
2 **onions**, chopped
⅔ cup **long-grain rice**
¼ cup **green lentils**
2 tablespoons finely chopped
cilantro
2 tablespoons finely chopped
parsley
salt and **black pepper**
plain yogurt and **cilantro
sprigs**, to garnish

Drain the chickpeas, rinse under cold running water,
and drain again. Place them in a saucepan, cover with
2 inches of water, and bring to a boil. Boil rapidly for
10 minutes, then lower the heat and simmer, partly
covered, for up to 1¾ hours, until tender, adding more
water as necessary. Drain and set aside.

Place the chicken breasts, stock, and water in a second
saucepan. Bring to a boil, lower the heat, cover the pan,
and simmer for 10–15 minutes or until the chicken is
just cooked. Remove the chicken from the stock, place
it on a board, and shred it, discarding the skin.

Set the shredded chicken aside. Add the chickpeas,
tomatoes, saffron (if using), onions, rice, and lentils to the
stock remaining in the pan. Cover the pan and simmer
for 30–35 minutes or until the rice and lentils are tender.

Add the shredded chicken, cilatnro, and parsley just
before serving. Heat the soup for another 5 minutes
without letting it boil. Season to taste and serve the soup,
garnished with drizzles of plain yogurt and cilantro sprigs.

For an economical harira, make up the soup as
above, omitting the chicken breasts and saffron and
adding ½ teaspoon of turmeric and ½ teaspoon of
ground cinnamon instead.

quick chicken soup

Serves **6**

Preparation time **10 minutes**

Cooking time **30 minutes**

20 cups (5 quarts) **water**

8 **chicken wings**

3 **tomatoes**

2 **Yukon gold** or **white round potatoes**, peeled and halved

1 large **onion**, halved

1 tied bunch of **flat-leaf parsley**

1 tied bunch of **cilantro**

¼ teaspoon **black pepper**

¼ teaspoon **ground turmeric**

¼ cup **short-grain rice**

salt

Put the water in a large, heavy flameproof casserole with the chicken wings, tomatoes, potatoes, onion, herbs, black pepper, turmeric, and salt to taste and bring to a boil. Cook for 25 minutes.

Remove the herbs. Remove and reserve the chicken wings.

Strain the vegetables, reserving the stock, and pass them through a food mill or blender until smooth.

Return the blended vegetables, the stock, and the chicken wings to the casserole and return to a boil. Add the rice in a steady stream, stir, and cook for another 5 minutes.

For chicken soup with rice, sauté 12 carrots (about 1½ lb), sliced, in 2 tablespoons butter over medium heat for 15 minutes. Add 5 cups chicken stock and 1 cup milk, bring to a boil, then simmer for 10 minutes, or until the carrots are tender. Process briefly to form a coarse consistency, then add 1 cup cooked rice and ½ tablespoon of crushed toasted cumin seeds. Heat through, then remove from the heat. Whisk in 2 egg yolks, then stir in 1 cup shredded cooked chicken breast and 2 tablespoons of chopped mint.

lamb & vegetable chorba

Serves **6**
Preparation time **20 minutes**
Cooking time **35 minutes**

4 cups **water**
8 oz **lamb**, cubed
1 **onion**, sliced in fine strips
¼ teaspoon **black pepper**
½ teaspoon **ground turmeric**
4 **carrots**, trimmed and cubed
2 **leeks**, trimmed and cubed
3 **Yukon gold** or **white round
  potatoes**, cubed
3 **turnips**, trimmed and cubed
2 **tomatoes**, cubed
1 bunch of **cilantro**, snipped
1 bunch of **flat-leaf parsley**,
  snipped
2 oz **vermicelli**
1 tablespoon **tomato paste**
2 tablespoons **butter**
salt

Bring the water to a boil in a large saucepan, then add the meat, onion, black pepper, turmeric, and salt to taste. Let cook for 20 minutes.

Add all the prepared vegetables. Add the snipped cilantro and parsley to the pan.

Let simmer for another 12 minutes, until the vegetables are cooked, then add the vermicelli and tomato paste and continue to cook for 8 minutes.

Stir in the butter just before serving.

For fish & vegetable chorba, omit the lamb. Make the recipe as above, adding 1 lb)firm white fish fillets, cut into chunks, with the vermicelli and tomato paste. Drizzle with 2 tablespoons of harissa to serve.

tagines

chicken with parsley

Serves **6**
Preparation time **15 minutes**
Cooking time **25 minutes**

3 tablespoons **olive oil**
1 large **onion**, finely chopped
3 **garlic cloves**, finely chopped
3 lb **chicken**, cut into pieces
pinch of **saffron**
1 cup **water**
2 large **tomatoes**
1 bunch of **flat-leaf parsley**,
  snipped
1 **preserved lemon**, cut into
  fine strips
3 cups pitted and rinsed
  green olives
¼ teaspoon **black pepper**
salt

Heat the oil in a large, heavy flameproof casserole and soften the onion and garlic.

Season the chicken pieces and add to the casserole, one at a time, and let brown on all sides for 5 minutes. Add the saffron and the water, cover the dish, and let cook over medium heat for 15 minutes.

Skin the tomatoes and cut into small pieces. Add to the casserole with the parsley and lemon, then lower the heat a little and let the sauce reduce slightly. Add the olives and season with the black pepper and salt.

Serve the chicken with the sauce and olives spooned around the sides.

For chicken with artichoke hearts, thaw 1 lb of frozen artichoke hearts, cut them into quarters, and add to the casserole when the chicken has been cooking for 10 minutes, with a little extra water, if necessary. Instead of using a whole bunch of parsley, use half parsley and half cilantro.

chicken with carrots

Serves **6**
Preparation time **20 minutes**
Cooking time **30 minutes**

3 lb **chicken**, cut into pieces
2 tablespoons **olive oil**
1 large **onion**, finely chopped
2 large **garlic cloves**, crushed
pinch of **saffron**
¼ teaspoon **ground turmeric**
¼ teaspoon **ground ginger**
1 cup **water**
2 lb **carrots**, trimmed and
    cut into sticks
1 tablespoon chopped
    flat-leaf parsley
1 **lemon**, juiced
pinch of **black pepper**
salt

Season the chicken.

Heat the oil in a large, heavy flameproof casserole
and brown the chicken pieces with the onion,
garlic, and spices.

Add the water and simmer over medium heat for
10 minutes, then add the carrots and cook for another
15 minutes.

Sprinkle with the parsley and the lemon juice when
the sauce has reduced slightly.

Remove from the heat after 5 minutes and season
with a pinch of black pepper and salt to taste.

For chicken with chestnuts, gently sauté 1 sliced
onion in 2 tablespoons of olive oil until soft and starting
to brown. Stir in ½ teaspoon each of ground cinnamon
and ginger and a pinch of saffron, then add the chicken
pieces and brown them all over. Add 1 cup of water
and simmer over medium heat for 25–30 minutes, until
the chicken is tender. Remove the chicken pieces, then
reduce the sauce. Stir in 1 tablespoon of honey, season
to taste, then add 2 (5 oz) packages roasted whole
chestnuts. Return the chicken to the casserole, adding
a little water, if necessary, and simmer for 4–5 minutes
to heat through.

moroccan chicken & harissa

Serves **4**
Preparation time **20 minutes**
Cooking time **35 minutes**

1 **onion**, finely chopped
2 teaspoons **paprika**
1 teaspoon **cumin seeds**
4 boneless, skinless **chicken
breasts**, about 4 oz each
1 bunch of **cilantro**, finely
chopped
¼ cup **lemon juice**
3 tablespoons **olive oil**
salt and **black pepper**

Harissa
4 **red bell peppers**
4 large **red chiles**
2 **garlic cloves**, crushed
½ teaspoon **coriander seeds**
1 teaspoon **caraway seeds**
⅓ cup **olive oil**

Make the harissa by heating a grill pan or skillet. Add the whole red bell peppers and cook for 15 minutes, turning occasionally. The skins will blacken and start to lift. Place the bell peppers in a plastic bag, seal the bag, and set aside (this encourages them to "sweat," making it easier to remove their skins). When cool enough to handle, remove the skin, cores, and seeds and place the flesh in a blender or food processor.

Remove the skin, cores, and seeds from the chiles in the same way and add the flesh to the blender with the garlic, coriander and caraway seeds, and olive oil. Process to a smooth paste. If not required immediately, place the harissa in a sealable container and pour a thin layer of olive oil over the top. Cover with a lid and refrigerate.

Clean the grill pan or skillet and reheat it. Place the onion in a bowl, add the paprika and cumin seeds, and mix together. Rub the onion-and-spice mixture into the chicken breasts. Cook the chicken for 10 minutes on each side, turning once. Remove from the pan.

Place the cilantro in a bowl and add the lemon juice, olive oil, and a little seasoning. Add the chicken to the bowl and toss well. Serve with rice and the harissa.

For spinach salad, to serve as an accompaniment, rinse and tear 1 (13 oz) package fresh spinach and add to a saucepan with any residual water. Cover and cook for 1–2 minutes, until wilted. Stir in 1 clove chopped garlic, ½ cup Greek yogurt, salt, and black pepper. Warm and serve.

chicken "mchermel"

Serves **6**
Preparation time **10 minutes**
Cooking time **25 minutes**

¼ cup **olive oil**
3 **onions,** finely chopped
3 lb **chicken,** cut into pieces
¼ teaspoon **ground turmeric**
pinch of **saffron**
¼ teaspoon **ground ginger**
1¾ cups **water**
4 **cilantro stems,** snipped
4 **parsley stems,** snipped
¼ teaspoon **ground cumin**
½ teaspoon **sweet paprika**
3 cups pitted and rinsed
  green olives
1 **lemon,** juiced
2 **preserved lemons,**
  to garnish
pinch of **black pepper**
salt

Heat the olive oil in a large, heavy flameproof casserole and brown the onions for 3 minutes.

Add the chicken pieces to the dish and season with the turmeric, saffron, ginger, black pepper, and salt to taste. Stir in 1¼ cups of the water, cover the pan, and let simmer over low heat for about 10 minutes.

Stir in the remaining water, the herbs, cumin, and paprika. Let reduce for about 10 minutes, until the sauce has thickened. Add the olives and lemon juice, and simmer for another 5 minutes.

Meanwhile, rinse the preserved lemons, cut them in half, and remove the pulp. Cut the rind into strips.

Transfer the chicken to a serving platter, pour the sauce around it, and garnish with the strips of preserved lemon.

For baked chicken with lemons, mix ½ teaspoon each of ground cinnamon and turmeric, plus seasoning to taste, and rub evenly over the chicken. Cook on all sides in 2 tablespoons of olive oil, then transfer to a lidded, flameproof casserole dish. Sauté a sliced large onion until soft, then stir in 2 teaspoons of grated fresh ginger root and 2½ cups hot chicken stock. Pour the mixture over the chicken. Cover and cook in a preheated oven, at 375°F, for 30 minutes. Add 2 preserved lemons cut into wedges, ¾ cup of olives, and 1 tablespoon of honey. Bake, uncovered, for another 45 minutes, until tender. Stir in ¼ cup of chopped cilantro to serve.

spicy stuffed chicken

Serves **6**
Preparation time **10 minutes**
Cooking time **1 hour 5 minutes**

3 **garlic cloves**, finely chopped
1 small **red chile**, sliced into
  thin rings
¼ cup **olive oil**
1 **lemon**, juiced
1 tablespoon **honey**
3 tablespoons **tomato juice**
1 tablespoon **ground cumin**
1 tablespoon **crushed Nora**
  peppercorns
1 tablespoon **ground ginger**
3 lb **chicken**
2 **bay leaves**
salt and **black pepper**

Stuffing
1¾ cups **raisins**
1 **garlic clove**, coarsely
  chopped
1 **onion**, coarsely chopped
2 tablespoons **butter**
½ teaspoon **ground cinnamon**
½ teaspoon **ground cumin**
2 tablespoons **blanched**
  almonds
salt and **black pepper**

Mix together the garlic, chile, oil, lemon juice, honey, tomato juice, and all the spices and stir well. Season to taste and set aside.

Make the stuffing by soaking the raisins in a little warm water. Puree the garlic and onion together in a blender. Melt the butter in a small saucepan and quickly brown the garlic and onion. Stir in the cinnamon and cumin and cook for about 2 minutes. Add the drained raisins and the almonds. Season and cook for another 2 minutes. Set aside to cool.

Preheat the oven to 425°F.

Fill the cavity of the chicken with the stuffing. Place in an ovenproof dish and brush with the sauce. Place the bay leaves on top. Roast for about 1 hour, basting from time to time with the cooking juices. Cut the chicken into pieces and serve hot with the stuffing and sauce.

For chicken with couscous stuffing, soak ½ cup chopped dried apricots in a little hot water. Prepare 1¼ cups instant couscous according to the package directions, adding 4 tablespoons of butter to the boiling water. Gently sauté 2 chopped onions in 2 tablespoons of butter until soft, then stir in 2 teaspoons of cinnamon and cook for another 2 minutes. Add the onions to the couscous with the apricots and 3 tablespoons of the soaking water, 2 tablespoons of sliced blanched almonds, and 1 tablespoon of honey. Season to taste, then fill the cavity of the chicken with the stuffing and cook as above.

roasted chicken with chermoula

Serves **6**

Preparation time **20 minutes**,
  plus marinating

Cooking time **45 minutes**

3 **garlic cloves**

1 bunch of **cilantro**

1 **lemon**, juiced

½ teaspoon **ground cumin**

¾ teaspoon **paprika**

pinch of **cayenne pepper**

3 tablespoons **sunflower oil**

½ teaspoon **salt**

3 **Cornish game hens**,
  cut in two

Make the chermoula marinade by chopping the garlic and cilantro together. Mix in a bowl with the lemon juice, spices, oil, and salt.

Coat the chicken with half the marinade and refrigerate for 1 hour.

Preheat the oven to 425°F.

Transfer the chicken to an ovenproof dish, drizzle with the remaining marinade, and cook for about 45 minutes.

For spring vegetables to serve as an accompaniment, bring 3 cups of chicken stock to a boil, then add 8 oz of baby carrots, 1¾ cups fava beans, and 6 sliced scallions. Cook for 8–10 minutes, until the carrots and fava beans are almost tender. Add 1¾ cups fresh young peas and cook for another 2 minutes. Stir in 2 tablespoons each of chopped cilantro and flat-leaf parsley and 1 tablespoon of chopped mint and season to taste.

chicken k'dra

Serves **4**

Preparation time **15 minutes**

Cooking time **2 hours
5 minutes**

2 tablespoons **olive oil**

8 boneless, skinless **chicken
thighs**, cut into large chunks

2 **onions**, thinly sliced

2 **garlic cloves**, finely chopped

2 tablespoons **all-purpose
flour**

3½ cups **chicken stock**

grated rind and juice of
1 **lemon**

2 large pinches **saffron
threads**

1 **cinnamon stick**, halved

2 (15 oz) cans **chickpeas**,
drained

4 **Yukon gold** or **white round
potatoes**, cut into chunks

salt and **black pepper**

parsley or **mixed parsley
and mint**, chopped, to
garnish

Heat the oil in a large skillet, add the chicken and onions, and cook, in batches if necessary, for 5 minutes, until golden.

Stir in the garlic, then mix in the flour. Add the stock, lemon rind and juice, saffron, cinnamon, and plenty of seasoning and bring to a boil.

Preheat the oven to 350°F.

Transfer to a tagine or casserole dish. Add the chickpeas and potatoes, mix together, then cover and cook for 2 hours.

Stir, then sprinkle with the herbs. Spoon into shallow bowls and serve with warm pita breads.

For saffron chicken with mixed vegetables, reduce the stock to 2½ cups and add 1 (14½ oz) can of diced tomatoes. Add only 1 (15 oz) can of chickpeas, then mix in 8 thickly sliced okra pods and 1 cup thickly sliced green beans 10 minutes before the end of cooking.

speedy spiced chicken tagine

Serves **4**
Preparation time **20 minutes**
Cooking time **55 minutes**

1 tablespoon **olive oil**
8 **chicken thighs**, skinned
1 **onion**, sliced
2 **garlic cloves**, finely chopped
8 **plum tomatoes**, skinned
   (optional), cut into chunks
1 teaspoon **ground turmeric**
1 **cinnamon stick**, halved
1 inch piece **fresh ginger root**,
   grated
2 teaspoons **honey**
¾ cup quartered **dried
   apricots**,
1 cup **couscous**
scant 2 cups boiling **water**
grated rind and juice of
   1 **lemon**
small bunch of **cilantro**,
   coarsely chopped
salt and **black pepper**

Heat the oil in a large skillet, add the chicken, and cook until browned on both sides. Lift out and transfer to a tagine or casserole dish. Add the onion to the skillet and sauté until golden.

Stir in the garlic, tomatoes, spices, and honey. Add the apricots and a little salt and black pepper and heat through. Spoon the mixture over the chicken, cover the dish, and bake in a preheated oven, at 350°F, for 45 minutes or until the chicken is cooked through.

When the chicken is almost ready, soak the couscous in boiling water for 5 minutes. Stir in the lemon rind and juice, cilantro, and seasoning. Spoon onto plates and top with the chicken and tomatoes, discarding the cinnamon stick just before eating.

For chicken & vegetable tagine, use just 4 chicken thighs and add 1 diced carrot, 1 cored, seeded, and diced red bell pepper, and 1 cup frozen fava beans. Replace the cinnamon with 2 teaspoons harissa paste and add ⅔ cup chicken stock. Cook as above, adding 8 thickly sliced okra pods or 1 cup green beans for the last 15 minutes of cooking. Sprinkle with chopped cilantro or mint and serve with rice.

quail with raisins

Serves **6**
Preparation time **10 minutes**
Cooking time **30 minutes**

2 tablespoons **sunflower oil**
5 tablespoons **butter**
3 large **onions**, finely chopped
12 small **quail**
1 **cinnamon stick**
¼ teaspoon **ground ginger**
pinch of **saffron**
⅔ cup **water**
2 cups **raisins**
½ teaspoon **ground cinnamon**
2 tablespoons **sugar**
2 tablespoons **honey**
¼ teaspoon **black pepper**
½ teaspoon **salt**

Heat the oil and half the butter in a large, heavy flameproof casserole and soften the onions.

Add the quail, cinnamon stick, ginger, saffron, and water and cook for 20 minutes.

Stir in the remaining butter, the raisins, ground cinnamon, sugar, honey, black pepper, and salt. Simmer until the sauce has reduced and has a caramel color.

For spiced vegetables to serve as an accompaniment, sauté 2 onions, cut into wedges, and 2 crushed garlic cloves in ¼ cup of olive oil until soft. Add 4 carrots, cut into large batons, and 2 fennel bulbs, cut into wedges, and cook for about 3 minutes until softened, then add 2 sliced zucchini and cook for another 2 minutes. Add 2 teaspoons of turmeric, 1 teaspoon of ground cumin, and ½ teaspoon of ground ginger and cook, stirring, for 1 minute. Stir in 2 large, ripe, peeled, and diced tomatoes and season to taste with salt and black pepper. Cover and cook over low heat, stirring occasionally, for about 10 minutes, or until the vegetables are just tender.

meatballs in tomato sauce

Serves **6**
Preparation time **15 minutes**
Cooking time **15 minutes**

1 **onion**, finely chopped
1 bunch of **flat-leaf parsley**,
  snipped
1 lb lean **ground beef** or
  ground lamb
1 tablespoon **paprika**
½ teaspoon **ground cumin**
3 tablespoons **peanut oil**
1¼ cups **tomato puree**
¼ teaspoon **tomato paste**
1 cup **water**
6 **eggs**
salt and **black pepper**

Place the onion and parsley in a large bowl with the meat, salt to taste, and half the paprika and cumin. Mix well and form into balls the size of a walnut. Set aside.

Pour the oil into a tagine and add the tomato puree, salt and black pepper to taste, and the remaining spices. Cook for 2 minutes, then add the tomato paste and water and cook until the sauce bubbles.

Place the meatballs carefully in the tagine and stir until they are sealed on all sides. Break the eggs over the meatballs and let bubble gently over low heat until the eggs are cooked.

Serve once the sauce has reduced.

For meatballs in spicy sun-dried tomato sauce,
first rehydrate 1 cup sun-dried tomatoes in boiling water, then process them in a food processor until smooth. Prepare the meatballs as above and set aside. Add the oil, tomato puree, and seasoning to the tagine with 3 crushed garlic cloves and a finely chopped red chile, the remaining paprika and cumin, and 1 teaspoon each of ground coriander and cinnamon. Cook for 2 minutes, then add the pureed sun-dried tomatoes, 1 cup well-flavored stock, and 2 tablespoons of chopped cilantro. Cook until the sauce bubbles, then complete the recipe as above.

moroccan lamb

Serves **2**

Preparation time **15 minutes**,
   plus marinating

Cooking time **1½ hours**

1 teaspoon **ground ginger**
1 teaspoon **ground cumin**
1 teaspoon **ground paprika**
1 **cinnamon stick**
¼ cup **orange juice**
8 oz lean **lamb**, cut into
   2 inch cubes
4 oz **pearl onions** or **shallots**,
   unpeeled
1 tablespoon **olive oil**
1 **garlic clove**, crushed
2 teaspoons **all-purpose flour**
2 teaspoons **tomato paste**
½ cup **lamb stock**
3 tablespoons **sherry**
⅓ cup **dried apricots**
1½ cup rinsed and drained,
   canned **chickpeas**
salt and **black pepper**
sprigs of **cilantro** or **flat-leaf
   parsley**, to garnish

Put the spices in a large bowl and pour the orange juice over them. Add the lamb and mix well, then cover and let sit in a cool place for at least 1 hour, or preferably overnight, in the refrigerator.

Put the onions or shallots in a heatproof bowl and cover with boiling water. Let sit for 2 minutes. Drain and refresh under cold water, then peel.

Heat the oil in a large, flameproof casserole. Remove the lamb from the marinade and pat dry with paper towels. Brown over high heat until golden all over. Using a slotted spoon, remove the lamb and set aside. Reduce the heat slightly and, adding a little more oil if necessary, cook the onions or shallots and garlic for 3 minutes or until just beginning to brown. Return the meat to the dish and stir in the flour and tomato paste. Cook for 1 minute.

Add the marinade to the casserole with the stock, sherry, and seasoning. Bring to a boil, then reduce the heat, cover, and place in a preheated oven, at 350°F, for 1 hour. Add the apricots and chickpeas and cook for another 15 minutes. Serve with couscous cooked according to the package directions and garnished with sprigs of cilantro or flat-leaf parsley.

For moroccan chicken, replace the lamb with the same quantity of chicken breast meat, cut into cubes, and cook as above. Replace the apricots with the same quantity of raisins.

lamb with orange & chickpeas

Serves **8**

Preparation time **25 minutes**, plus overnight soaking

Cooking time **2½ hours**

1¼ cups **chickpeas**, soaked in cold water overnight

¼ cup **olive oil**

2 teaspoons **ground cumin**

1 teaspoon each **ground cinnamon**, **ground ginger**, and **ground turmeric**

½ teaspoon **saffron threads**

3 lb **shoulder of lamb**, trimmed of all fat and cut into 1 inch cubes

2 **onions**, coarsely chopped

3 **garlic cloves**, finely chopped

2 **tomatoes**, skinned, seeded, and chopped

12 pitted **ripe black olives**, sliced

grated rind of 1 **unwaxed lemon**

grated rind of 1 **unwaxed orange**

⅓ cup chopped **cilantro**

salt and **black pepper**

Drain and rinse the chickpeas. Place them in a large saucepan and cover with water. Bring to a boil, then cover and simmer for about 1–1½ hours, until tender.

Meanwhile, combine half the olive oil with the cumin, cinnamon, ginger, turmeric, and saffron in a large bowl, plus ½ teaspoon each salt and black pepper. Add the cubed lamb, toss, and set aside in a cool place for 20 minutes. Wipe out the pan, heat the remaining oil, and cook the lamb, in batches, until browned; transfer to a plate to drain.

Add the onions to the pan and cook, stirring constantly, until browned. Add the garlic, tomatoes, and 1 cup of water, stirring and scraping the bottom of the pan. Return the lamb to the pan and add water to just cover. Bring to a boil, skim off any surface foam, then cover and simmer for about 1 hour or until the meat is tender.

Drain the chickpeas, reserving the cooking liquid. Add the chickpeas and about 1 cup of the cooking liquid to the lamb. Simmer for 30 minutes. Stir in the olives, lemon rind, and orange rind and simmer for 30 minutes. Stir in half the cilantro, using the remainder to garnish.

For easy lamb tagine, place 3 lb cubed shoulder of lamb in a saucepan with 1 teaspoon of salt, cover with water, and bring slowly to a boil. Skim and add a pinch of saffron, 1 whole, unpeeled onion, and 1½ teaspoons each of crushed coriander seeds and black peppercorns. Simmer for 2 hours, then discard the onion. Cool the stock and skim the fat, then add ½ teaspoon of turmeric and the juice of 2 small oranges and reheat gently.

lamb & prune tagine with barley

Serves **4**
Preparation time **15 minutes**
Cooking time **1–1¼ hours**

olive oil spray
1¼ lb lean diced **lamb**
1 **red onion**, chopped
1 **carrot**, peeled and chopped
1 teaspoon **paprika**
1 teaspoon **ground coriander**
1 teaspoon **fennel seeds**
1¼ inch **cinnamon stick**
2 **garlic cloves**, crushed
2 **bay leaves**
2 tablespoons **lime juice**
3 cups **chicken stock**
8 **dried prunes**
1 (14½ oz) can **diced
  tomatoes**
⅓ cup **pearl barley**
⅓ cup chopped **cilantro**, plus
  extra sprigs to garnish
1 tablespoon **lime juice**,
  to garnish
2 cups **couscous**
salt and **black pepper**

Heat a large saucepan or 2 quart flameproof casserole, spray lightly with oil, and cook the lamb briefly, in batches if necessary, until brown. Remove the lamb with a slotted spoon, add the onion and carrot to the pan, and cook briefly to brown. Return the lamb, stir in all the remaining ingredients, and season to taste.

Simmer, covered, for 1 hour or until the lamb is tender. At the end of the cooking time, stir in the cilantro and lime juice.

Meanwhile, cook the couscous according to the package directions and set aside for 5 minutes.

Serve the hot tagine spooned over the couscous and garnished with cilantro sprigs.

For pork & apricot tagine, replace the lamb with the same quantity of diced pork and replace the dried prunes with dried apricots. Toast a generous handful of slivered almonds in a dry saucepan over medium heat, then stir into the casserole along with the other ingredients.

lamb with quince

Serves **6**

Preparation time **20 minutes**

Cooking time **30 minutes**

2½ lb l**eg of lamb** or
    shoulder of lamb, cubed

2 **onions**, finely chopped

1 cup **water**

2 tablespoons **peanut oil**

4 tablespoons **butter**

1 **cinnamon stick**

pinch of **saffron**

½ teaspoon **ground ginger**

10 **quince** (about 2 lb)

½ teaspoon **ground cinnamon**

2 tablespoons **sugar**

2 tablespoons **honey**

pinch of **black pepper**

salt

Place the lamb and onions in a large, heavy flameproof casserole with the water, oil, half the butter, the cinnamon stick, saffron, and ginger. Season, then cover the dish and cook over medium heat for 20 minutes.

Meanwhile, peel and core the quince and cut into eighths. Put the remaining butter, the ground cinnamon, sugar, and honey in a saucepan and moisten with 2 ladlefuls of the cooking juices from the casserole.

Add the quince and cook until they are caramelized.

Transfer the meat to a round serving plate and serve with the sauce and the quince.

For lamb with quince & caramelized shallots,

use only 1 chopped onion when cooking the meat. Blanch 1 lb of shallots in boiling water for 5 minutes. When cool enough to handle, peel and trim the shallots and sauté them in 2 tablespoons of peanut oil for 5–10 minutes, until starting to brown. Caramelize with the quince, adding more of the meat cooking juices if necessary.

moroccan meatball tagine

Serves **4**
Preparation time **15 minutes**
Cooking time **40 minutes**

2 small **onions**, finely chopped
2 tablespoons **raisins**
1 ½ lb **ground beef**
1 tablespoon **tomato paste**
3 teaspoons **curry powder**
3 tablespoons **olive oil**
½ teaspoon **ground cinnamon**
2⅔ cups canned **diced
  tomatoes**
½ **lemon**, juiced
2 **celery sticks**, thickly sliced
1 large or 2 medium
  zucchini, coarsely chopped
1 ¼ cups **frozen peas**

Mix together half the onions, the raisins, ground beef, tomato paste, and curry powder in a bowl. Using your hands, knead to combine the mixture evenly. Form the mixture into 24 meatballs.

Heat 1 tablespoon of the oil in a saucepan, add the meatballs, in small batches, and cook until browned all over. Drain out the excess fat and put all the meatballs in the pan. Add the cinnamon, tomatoes, and lemon juice, cover, and simmer gently for 25 minutes, until the meatballs are cooked.

Meanwhile, heat the remaining oil in a large skillet, add the celery and zucchini, and cook until soft and starting to brown. Add the peas and cook for another 5 minutes, until the peas are tender.

Stir the zucchini mixture into the meatball mixture just before serving.

For cilantro & apricot couscous to serve as an accompaniment, put 1 cup instant couscous in a large, heatproof bowl with ⅓ cup chopped dried apricots. Pour boiling hot vegetable stock over the couscous to just cover the grains. Cover and let sit for 10–12 minutes, until all the water has been absorbed. Meanwhile, chop 2 large, ripe tomatoes and finely chop 2 tablespoons cilantro leaves. Fluff up the couscous with a fork and transfer to a warm serving dish. Stir in the tomatoes, cilantro, and 2 tablespoons of olive oil, and season to taste. Toss well to mix and serve with the tagine.

lamb with apricots

Serves **6**
Preparation time **20 minutes**
Cooking time **1¼ hours**

1 **orange**
1 cup **dried apricots**
2 tablespoons **olive oil**
1 large **onion**, finely sliced
2½ lb **shoulder of lamb**,
   cubed
½ teaspoon **ground cumin**
¼ teaspoon **ground cinnamon**
1 tablespoon **ground almonds**
   (almond meal)
1¼ cups **water**
1 tablespoon **white sesame**
   seeds
½ bunch of **cilantro**, snipped
   (optional)
salt and **black pepper**

Wash the orange, then zest the rind. Squeeze the juice and soak the apricots in the juice to swell.

Heat the oil in a large, heavy flameproof casserole and brown the onion for about 10 minutes, stirring from time to time.

Add the meat, cumin, cinnamon, and salt and black pepper to taste, and stir well for 5 minutes. Pour in the orange juice with the apricots, orange rind, almonds, and water. Cover and bring to a simmer over medium heat. When the liquid is bubbling, lower the heat and continue to cook, stirring from time to time, for about 40 minutes, or until the lamb is cooked.

Meanwhile, dry-toast the sesame seeds in a skillet. They should become golden but not blackened.

Transfer the cooked lamb to a serving platter and sprinkle with the sesame seeds and cilantro, if using.

For zucchini puree to serve as an accompaniment, thickly slice 3 medium zucchini and steam until tender. Drain, chop, and mash them well in a colander to release the juices. Heat 2 tablespoons of olive oil in a large skillet and soften 8 plum tomatoes with 6 sliced garlic cloves over medium heat. When the garlic begins to brown, add the zucchini puree, season to taste with salt and black pepper, and stir in 2 tablespoons of chopped cilantro. Serve drizzled with olive oil.

lamb with mushrooms

Serves **6**
Preparation time **15 minutes**
Cooking time **25 minutes**

¼ cup **olive oil**
2½ lb)**leg of lamb** or
shoulder of lamb, cubed
1 **onion**, finely chopped
2 **garlic cloves**, finely chopped
1½ cups **water**
½ teaspoon **ground ginger**
pinch of **saffron**
1½ lb **cremini mushrooms**,
peeled and sliced
1 (3 oz) jar of **porcini**
mushrooms in white truffle
paste or 3½ cups **white**
truffles (optional)
½ bunch of **flat-leaf parsley**,
snipped
½ bunch of **cilantro**, snipped
salt and **black pepper**
chopped **cilantro** or **flat-leaf**
parsley, to garnish

Heat the olive oil in a large, heavy flameproof casserole and cook the meat, onion, and garlic for 2 minutes.

Add the water, ginger, saffron, and salt and black pepper to taste. Cover and cook for 15 minutes.

Stir in the cremini mushrooms (along with the porcini mushrooms in white truffle paste, if using), and the parsley and cilantro. Let simmer over low heat for another 5–7 minutes, until the sauce has reduced.

Transfer to a serving platter, with the meat arranged around the mushrooms and garnished with chopped cilantro or flat-leaf parsley.

For pomegranate lamb, heat ¼ cup of olive oil and briefly sauté 3 crushed cardamom seeds, 3 cloves, and 1 teaspoon of fenugreek seeds. Remove the spices, then add 2½ lb cubed lamb, 1 finely chopped onion, 2 finely chopped garlic cloves, and ½ teaspoon of ground ginger. Cook for 2 minutes to brown the meat, then gradually stir in 1½ cups pomegranate juice. Add ½ teaspoon each of ground cumin, cinnamon, and mace, season with salt and black pepper, and cook for another 1 minute. Stir in ⅓ cup of plain yogurt, then cover and cook over low heat for about 30 minutes, or until the meat is tender, stirring occasionally and adding a little water, if necessary.

rabbit in spicy sauce

Serves **6**
Preparation time **15 minutes**
Cooking time **25 minutes**

1 prepared **rabbit**, cut into
    8 pieces
3 tablespoons **olive oil**
1 large **onion**, chopped
3 **garlic cloves**, crushed
1 tablespoon **paprika**
½ teaspoon **ground cumin**
pinch of **cayenne pepper**
¼ teaspoon **black pepper**
1¼ cups **water**
2 tablespoons **white wine**
    vinegar
kosher salt

Rub the rabbit pieces with the salt. Soak in water
for several minutes.

Heat the oil in a flameproof casserole and soften the
onion and garlic for 2 minutes. Add the drained rabbit
and the spices.

Pour in the water and simmer over low heat for
20 minutes to reduce the sauce.

Remove from the heat and stir in the vinegar.

For rabbit tagine with prunes, follow the recipe as
above, replacing the paprika, cumin, and cayenne with
½ teaspoon each of ground ginger and cinnamon. Add
8 chopped dried prunes and 1 tablespoon of honey to
the sauce 5 minutes before the end of cooking time,
and stir in the juice of 1 lemon instead of the vinegar.

chickpea tagine

Serves **4**
Preparation time **15 minutes**
Cooking time **40 minutes**

½ cup **extra-virgin olive oil**
1 large **onion**, finely chopped
2 **garlic cloves**, crushed
2 teaspoons **ground coriander**
1 teaspoon each **ground
cumin, ground cinnamon,
and ground turmeric**
1 large **eggplant**, (about
12 oz), diced
1 (15 oz) can **chickpeas**,
drained
1 (14½ oz) can **diced
tomatoes**
1¼ cups **vegetable stock**
4 cups **white button
mushrooms**
½ cup chopped **dried figs**
2 tablespoons chopped
cilantro
salt and **black pepper**
preserved lemon, chopped,
to garnish

Heat 2 tablespoons of the oil in a saucepan, add the onion, garlic, and spices, and cook over medium heat, stirring frequently, for 5 minutes, until lightly golden. Heat another 2 tablespoons of the oil in the pan, add the eggplants, and cook, stirring, for 4–5 minutes, until browned. Add the chickpeas, tomatoes, and stock and bring to a boil. Reduce the heat, cover, and simmer gently for 20 minutes.

Meanwhile, heat the remaining oil in a skillet, add the mushrooms, and cook over medium heat for 4–5 minutes, until browned.

Add the mushrooms to the tagine with the figs and cook for another 10 minutes. Stir in the cilantro. Garnish with chopped preserved lemon.

For butternut squash tagine, soften 2 sliced onions in 2 tablespoons of olive oil in a large saucepan. Stir in 2 teaspoons each of ground cumin and coriander and 2 crushed garlic cloves and cook for 2 minutes, then add 2 tablespoons of rose harissa and cook for another 3 minutes. Add 1 butternut squash and 4 carrots, peeled and cut into chunks, and cook, stirring constantly, for 10 minutes. Stir in ½ cup chopped dried apricots and pour 2½ cups of vegetable stock over the mixture. Cook gently for 20–25 minutes, or until the vegetables are almost tender. Add 1 (15 oz) can of drained chickpeas and cook for another 5 minutes. Season to taste with salt and black pepper and stir in 2 tablespoons each of cilantro and flat-leaf parsley to serve.

chickpea & potato tagine

Serves **4**
Preparation time **15 minutes**
Cooking time **46 minutes**
Finishing time **10 minutes**

2 tablespoons **sunflower oil**
2 **onions**, coarsely chopped
1 teaspoon **smoked paprika**
1 teaspoon **ground turmeric**
2 teaspoons **cumin seeds**,
  coarsely crushed
4 **Yukon gold** or **white round
  potatoes**, scrubbed and
  cubed
1 (15 oz) can **chickpeas**,
  drained
1 (15 oz) can **pinto beans**,
  rinsed and drained
1 **preserved lemon**, drained
  and quartered
2½ cups **vegetable stock**
small bunch of **cilantro**
1 cup crumbled **feta cheese**
  (optional)
salt and **black pepper**

Heat the oil in a saucepan, add the onion, and sauté for
5 minutes, until lightly browned. Stir in the spices and
cook for 1 minute. Mix in the potatoes and drained
chickpeas and beans and stir well.

Add the preserved lemon, stock, and seasoning. Bring to
a boil, then reduce the heat, cover, and simmer gently for
40 minutes, until the potatoes are tender. Let cool, then
chill until required.

To serve, reheat the potato mixture on the stove, stirring
occasionally and topping up with a little water, if needed,
until piping hot. Spoon into shallow bowls and top with
torn cilantro leaves and feta cheese, if using. Serve with
warmed pita breads or flatbreads, if desired.

For lentil & fennel tagine, gently soften 12 peeled
baby shallots in 2 tablespoons of olive oil. Add ¾ cup
green lentils, 1 cup chopped dried apricots, 2 crushed
garlic cloves, a 1½ inch piece of fresh ginger root, finely
grated, 2 teaspoons of ras el hanout, and ½ teaspoon
of ground cumin. Cook for another 2 minutes, then pour
n 3½ cups vegetable stock. Bring to a boil, then cover
and simmer over low heat for 15 minutes. Add 12 baby
carrots, 2 fennel bulbs cut into wedges, and 2 sliced
zucchini and cook for another 5 minutes. Add 1⅓ cups
fresh peas and the grated rind of 1 lemon and cook
for another 5 minutes. Stir in the juice of 1 lemon and
season with salt and black pepper.

fish

spliced sardines

Serves **6**

Preparation time **15 minutes**, plus marinating

Cooking time **15 minutes**

36 **sardines**
4 **garlic cloves**
½ bunch of **flat-leaf parsley**
1 large bunch of **cilantro**
1 **lemon**, juiced
1 tablespoon **paprika**
1 tablespoon **ground cumin**
pinch of **cayenne pepper**
¾ cup **all-purpose flour**
½ teaspoon **salt**
oil for frying
lemon wedges, to serve

Fillet and butterfly the sardines (or ask your fish dealer to do this when you buy them).

Rinse the sardines and let them drain while you prepare the marinade. Chop the garlic, parsley, and cilantro, transfer to a large bowl, and add the lemon juice, salt, and the spices.

Coat the fillets with marinade on both sides, then press them together in pairs, open sides together. Lay on a plate, drizzle with the remaining marinade, cover with plastic wrap, and marinate in the refrigerator for 1 hour.

Heat the oil in a large skillet, dredge the sardines with flour on both sides, and cook over low heat, turning once. Transfer to paper towels to absorb the excess oil before arranging on a serving platter.

For sardine balls with chermoula, to make the chermoula, mix together ½ cup olive oil, the juice of 1 lemon, ¼ cup each of chopped flat-leaf parsley and cilantro, 4 crushed garlic cloves, 1 teaspoon each of ground cumin and paprika, and salt and black pepper to taste. Finely chop 2 lb sardine fillets in a food processor, then mix with 2 tablespoons of cooked rice and enough chermoula to bind. Form the mixture into little balls. Simmer 6 peeled and chopped, ripe tomatoes with the remaining chermoula and a bay leaf, until reduced. Add the sardine balls and 2 tablespoons of water and cook, stirring occasionally, for another 15 minutes.

118

stuffed squid

Serves **6**

Preparation time **15 minutes**

Cooking time **20 minutes**

6 medium **squid** (about
  5 inches long)
1 bunch of **flat-leaf parsley**
1 bunch of **cilantro**
5 oz **ground beef**
½ cup **cooked rice**
¼ teaspoon **black pepper**
1 tablespoon **paprika**
½ cup **tomato puree**
2 tablespoons **olive oil**
2 **garlic cloves**, sliced
¼ teaspoon **ground cumin**
1 cup **water**
½ teaspoon **tomato paste**
salt

Wash and clean the squid and set aside. Wash and snip the parsley and cilantro separately.

Mix together the meat, parsley, rice, salt to taste, black pepper, and half the paprika in a large bowl.

Stuff the squid pouches and secure with a toothpick.

Put the tomato puree into a large flameproof casserole with the oil, garlic, cilantro, cumin, and the remaining paprika. Pour in the water and bring to a simmer. Add the squid and the tomato paste, cover, and simmer for 20 minutes. The squid should be tender and the sauce reduced.

For squid with shrimp & harissa, clean the squid, cut into thin strips, and season with salt and black pepper. Sauté with 1 lb shrimp in ⅓ cup of olive oil over high heat, stirring occasionally, for about 1 minute, or until the squid is just opaque and the shrimp are pink. Stir in ⅓ cup of harissa (see page 76) and ¼ cup of chopped cilantro and serve immediately.

shrimp "pil-pil"

Serves **6**
Preparation time **5 minutes**
Cooking time **10 minutes**

¼ cup **peanut oil**
1 lb **jumbo shrimp**, shelled
  and deveined
2 **garlic cloves**, coarsely
  chopped
1 tablespoon snipped
  flat-leaf parsley
½ teaspoon **paprika**
½ teaspoon **salt**
2 fresh **red chiles**, to garnish

Heat the oil in a skillet or flameproof tagine over medium heat.

Add the shrimp, garlic, parsley, paprika, and salt. Stir gently, turning to cook on both sides, then add the chiles to garnish the dish. Serve hot.

For shrimp in tomato sauce, sauté a chopped onion in 2 tablespoons of olive oil until just starting to brown. Add 3 finely chopped garlic cloves; when they start to brown, stir in 2⅓ cups peeled and chopped tomatoes, ½ teaspoon of ground ginger, a pinch of chili powder, and a pinch of salt. Simmer for 20 minutes or until the sauce is reduced. Add the shrimp, turning to cook on both sides. Season to taste with salt and black pepper, then stir in 1 tablespoon each of chopped parsley and cilantro.

fried whiting with chermoula

Serves **6**
Preparation time **15 minutes**,
  plus marinating
Cooking time **15 minutes**

6 whole **whiting** or 12 fillets
1 bunch of **cilantro**, snipped
1 bunch of **flat-leaf parsley**,
  snipped
2 **garlic cloves**, crushed
½ teaspoon **sweet paprika**
½ teaspoon **ground cumin**
1 **lemon**, juiced
1 tablespoon **water**
¼ cup **flour**
½ teaspoon **salt**
oil, for frying
lemon wedges, to serve

Wash the whole or filleted fish.

Prepare the marinade in a shallow dish by mixing together the herbs, garlic, spices, lemon juice, and water.

Place the fish in the marinade, cover with plastic wrap, and let marinate for 30 minutes in the refrigerator.

Put the flour onto a plate and dip in the fish to coat both sides. Reserve the remaining flour and the marinade.

Heat the oil in a skillet large enough to accommodate the whiting and quickly cook the fish, turning once. You may have to work in batches.

Remove the fish and keep warm. Mix the remaining flour with the marinade and shape into flat patties. Cook in the hot oil and serve with the fish.

For deep-fried fish with chermoula sauce, mix the juice of 1½ lemons with a generous handful of chopped cilantro, 2 crushed garlic cloves, ½ a finely chopped red chile, ⅓ cup of olive oil, and salt to taste. Dip 6 white fish fillets in flour as above and quickly deep-fry them, in batches, until golden. Serve hot, with the sauce poured over the fish.

moroccan fish tagine

Serves **4**
Preparation time **15 minutes**
Cooking time **55 minutes**

1 ½ lb **firm white fish fillets**,
  such as cod, sea bass, or
  monkfish, pin boned, skinned,
  and cut into 2 inch chunks
½ teaspoon **cumin seeds**
½ teaspoon **coriander seeds**
6 **cardamom pods**
¼ cup **olive oil**
2 small **onions**, thinly sliced
2 **garlic cloves**, crushed
¼ teaspoon **ground turmeric**
1 **cinnamon stick**
¼ cup **golden raisins**
3 tablespoons **pine nuts**,
  lightly toasted
⅔ cup **fish stock**
finely grated rind of 1 **lemon**,
  plus 1 tablespoon juice
salt and **black pepper**
chopped **parsley**, to garnish

Season the fish with salt and black pepper.

Using a mortar and pestle, crush the cumin and coriander seeds and cardamom pods. Discard the cardamom pods, leaving the seeds.

Heat the oil in a large, shallow skillet and sauté the onions gently for 6–8 minutes, until golden. Add the garlic, crushed spices, turmeric, and cinnamon and sauté gently, stirring, for 2 minutes. Add the fish pieces, turning them until they are coated in the oil. Transfer the fish and onions to an ovenproof casserole and sprinkle with the golden raisins and pine nuts.

Add the stock and lemon rind and juice to the skillet and bring the mixture to a boil. Pour the mixture around the fish, then cover and bake in a preheated oven, at 325°F, for 40 minutes. Garnish with parsley before serving.

For pomegranate & cilantro couscous to serve as an accompaniment, bring 1 ¾ cups vegetable stock to a boil. Pour it over 1 ½ cups couscous in a heatproof bowl, cover with plastic wrap, and let steam for 5 minutes, then stir in the seeds of 1 pomegranate and 2 tablespoons of coarsely chopped cilantro leaves. Mix in 2 tablespoons of olive oil and the juice of ½ lemon, then season with salt and black pepper.

hake with saffron

Serves **6**

Preparation time **10 minutes**

Cooking time **15 minutes**

1 bunch of **cilantro**

4 **garlic cloves**

½ teaspoon **ground ginger**

½ teaspoon **ground turmeric**

2 pinches of **saffron threads**

6 **hake, whiting,** or **cod steaks**

3 tablespoons **olive oil**

½ cup **water**

1 **tomato**, skinned and chopped finely

1 **preserved lemon**, sliced into strips

salt

lemon slices, to garnish

Finely mince together the cilantro and the garlic. Put in a bowl with the spices. Coat the fish with the spice mixture and set aside.

Pour the oil and water into a large flameproof casserole. Place over the heat and bring to a gentle boil before carefully lowering in the fish. Cook over low heat for about 15 minutes.

Add the tomato and the preserved lemon to the dish. When the sauce is thick, remove the casserole from the heat and carefully lift out the fish.

Serve with the sauce spooned on top.

For saffron fish balls, process to a thick paste 1 lb white fish fillets, 1 egg, 2 chopped scallions, 1 tablespoon each of chopped cilantro and flat-leaf parsley, 1 cup fresh white bread crumbs, a large pinch of saffron, and seasoning to taste. Shape the mixture into walnut-size balls and set aside. Sauté a finely chopped onion in ¼ cup of olive oil until soft. Stir in 4 peeled and chopped tomatoes, 2 crushed garlic cloves, 1 tablespoon of harissa, 1 teaspoon of paprika, ½ teaspoon of ground cumin, and a pinch of sugar. Add 1 cup of water, bring to a boil, then simmer for 15 minutes. Add the fish balls and simmer, covered, for another 15 minutes, shaking the pan occasionally.

stuffed red porgy

Serves **6**

Preparation time **15 minutes**

Cooking time **1 hour
5 minutes**

3 lb **porgy,** cleaned and scaled

14 oz **hake fillet**

1 bunch of **flat-leaf parsley**

2 **celery sticks**

1 **red bell pepper**

1 **preserved lemon**

3 **garlic cloves**

2 tablespoons **sunflower oil**

1⅔ cups **cooked rice**

½ teaspoon **ground turmeric**

pinch of **saffron**

½ teaspoon **ground ginger**

1 **lemon**, juiced

2 tablespoons **olive oil**

1 cup **water**

pinch of **black pepper**

salt

Wash the porgy thoroughly. Mince together the hake, parsley, celery, bell pepper, preserved lemon, and garlic. Heat 1 tablespoon of the sunflower oil in a skillet, add the mixture, and cook over low heat, stirring, for 3 minutes. Remove from the skillet and let cool.

Put the rice, spices, and half the lemon juice in a bowl, then add the cooled hake mixture and combine.

Preheat the oven to 350°F.

Rub the porgy with the remaining lemon juice, season with salt and black pepper, and drizzle with the remaining olive oil, then fill with the stuffing. Put the remaining sunflower and olive oil in a shallow ovenproof dish, pour in the water, and place the stuffed fish in the casserole. Transfer to the oven and cook for 1 hour.

For porgy with new potatoes, mix ⅓ cup of olive oil with the juice of 1 lemon, ¼ cup of chopped cilantro, 4 crushed garlic cloves, 1 teaspoon each of ground cumin and paprika, and ½ teaspoon of chile. Sprinkle 6 porgy fillets with salt and marinate in half the chermoula. Cut 2 lb new potatoes into thin slices and 4 large, firm tomatoes into slightly thicker slices. Toss gently in 2 tablespoons of olive oil, season to taste, then transfer to an oiled ovenproof dish. Bake in a preheated oven, at 475°F, turning occasionally, for about 45 minutes, until tender. Place the fish fillets on top, skin side up, and bake for another 10 minutes, or until the fish is cooked. Serve drizzled with the remaining chermoula.

sea bass with celery

Serves 6
Preparation time **15 minutes**
Cooking time **1 hour**

3 lb **sea bass**, cleaned and
   scaled
1 bunch of **celery**
1 ¼ cups **tomato puree**
½ teaspoon **sweet paprika**
½ teaspoon **black pepper**
¼ cup **olive oil**
3 **garlic cloves**
1 cup **water**
salt
couscous, to serve

Wash the sea bass thoroughly and set aside. Separate and wash the celery sticks, reserving the leafy parts. Remove the strings and cut the sticks into pieces about 1 ½ inches in length. Bring a large saucepan of salted water to a boil and blanch the celery for 2 minutes. Meanwhile, finely chop the reserved leafy parts.

Put the tomato puree into a skillet with the paprika, black pepper, a little salt, and half the olive oil. Heat gently for 10 minutes, then add the blanched celery and leafy parts and continue to cook for another 10 minutes. Remove from the heat and let cool.

Preheat the oven to 350°F.

Put half the tomato sauce in the bottom of an ovenproof dish that will accommodate the fish and place the sea bass on top. Drizzle with the remaining olive oil and the rest of the sauce, then add the water. Mix well, then cook in the preheated oven for about 45 minutes. Serve with couscous.

For sea bass with herbs, make the tomato sauce as above, omitting the paprika. Mix together ⅓ cup each of chopped cilantro and flat-leaf parsley, 3 crushed garlic cloves, and the finely grated rind and juice of 1 ½ lemons. Season to taste with salt and black pepper and use to stuff the fish. Cook the fish with the sauce as above.

porgy with olives

Serves **6**
Preparation time **20 minutes**
Cooking time **1 hour**

4 lb **porgy,** cleaned and scaled
3 **tomatoes,** skinned and cut
    into small pieces
3 **celery sticks,** finely chopped
1 bunch of **flat-leaf parsley,**
    finely chopped
2 **preserved lemons,**
    quartered, pulp removed,
    and rind finely sliced
3 **garlic cloves,** minced
5 **white round potatoes,**
    sliced
½ teaspoon **turmeric**
½ teaspoon **black pepper**
1½ cups **cooked rice**
2½ cups pitted **green olives**
3 tablespoons **olive oil**
salt

Wash the fish thoroughly, then slash twice on both sides.

Prepare a marinade with the tomatoes, celery, parsley, lemon rind, garlic, turmeric, black pepper, salt to taste, and a large glass of water. Add half the mixture to the cooked rice with half the olives. Fill the fish cavity with this stuffing.

Preheat the oven to 350°F.

Pour the oil and the remaining marinade into a roasting pan and place the fish in the middle with the sliced potatoes around it. Stir well to coat the potatoes in the marinade. Transfer to the oven and cook for 1 hour. Serve garnished with the remaining olives.

For skate with olives, heat ⅓ cup of olive oil in a large skillet and gently cook 6 small skate wings on one side for 4 minutes. Turn the fish over and continue cooking until the flesh is opaque and readily comes away from the bones. Remove from the skillet and keep warm. (Do this in two batches, if necessary.) Stir into the skillet the juice of 1½ lemons, the chopped peel of 2 small preserved lemons, 18 pitted and chopped green olives, and 3 tablespoons of chopped cilantro. Heat through gently and pour the sauce over the fish to serve.

moroccan broiled sardines

Serves **4**
Preparation time **10 minutes**
Cooking time **6–8 minutes**

12 **sardines**, cleaned and
  gutted
2 tablespoons **harissa**
2 tablespoons **olive oil**
1 **lemon**, juiced
salt flakes and **black pepper**
chopped **cilantro**, to garnish
lemon wedges, to serve

Heat the broiler on the hottest setting. Rinse the sardines and pat dry with paper towels. Make 3 deep slashes on both sides of each fish with a sharp knife.

Mix the harissa with the oil and lemon juice to make a thin paste. Rub into the sardines on both sides. Put the sardines on a lightly oiled baking sheet. Cook under the broiler for 3–4 minutes on each side, depending on their size, or until cooked through.

Season to taste with salt flakes and black pepper and serve immediately garnished with cilantro and with lemon wedges for squeezing over.

For baked sardines with pesto, line a medium ovenproof dish with 2 sliced tomatoes and 2 sliced onions. Prepare the sardines as above, then rub ¼ cup of pesto over the fish and arrange in a single layer on top of the tomatoes and onions. Cover with aluminum foil and bake in a preheated oven, at 400°F, for 20–25 minutes or until the fish is cooked through.

tangiers-style anchovies

Serves **6**
Preparation time **35 minutes**
Cooking time **10 minutes**

2 lb **anchovies**
6 **garlic cloves**, chopped
1 bunch of **flat-leaf parsley**,
  finely chopped
1 bunch of **cilantro**,
  finely chopped
2 tablespoons **paprika**
2 tablespoons **ground cumin**
¼ cup **vinegar**
2 tablespoons **water**
¼ cup **olive oil**
2 tablespoons ground **thyme**

Wash the anchovies and remove the spine to make two fillets without separating them. Lay them flat in a bowl.

Preheat the oven to 350°F.

Prepare a marinade with all the ingredients except the olive oil and ground thyme. Dip each prepared anchovy on both sides first in the marinade, then in the olive oil. Close the two fillets together, and arrange them in a single layer in a roasting pan or tagine. Pour the remaining marinade over the anchovies and sprinkle with the thyme.

Transfer the pan to the oven for 10 minutes or place the tagine over low heat.

For roasted peppers with anchovies, place 6 halved and seeded red bell peppers in an ovenproof dish and coat all over with olive oil. Arrange, cut side up, on a baking pan and roast in a preheated oven, at 325°F, for 35–40 minutes or until softened. Fill each roasted pepper half with ½ a tomato, 2 or 3 slices of garlic, ¼ teaspoon of finely chopped preserved lemon, a sprig of rosemary, and 2 anchovies, split lengthwise. Drizzle the peppers with olive oil and return to the oven for another 30 minutes or until the tomatoes are soft. Serve at room temperature.

kebabs &
accompaniments

beef kebabs

Serves **6**
Preparation time **15 minutes**,
  plus resting
Cooking time **5 minutes**

2¼ lb **tenderloin steak**, cubed
1 large **onion**, chopped
1 bunch of **flat-leaf parsley**,
  snipped
¼ teaspoon **black pepper**
salt

Mix together all the ingredients in a bowl and season with salt.

Cover with plastic wrap and place in the refrigerator for 1 hour.

Thread the steak onto 6 skewers and cook for 5 minutes, turning regularly, over hot coals or under a preheated hot broiler.

For sweet tomato sauce to serve as an accompaniment, gently heat 2 tablespoons of olive oil with 2 sliced garlic cloves for 3 minutes. Remove the garlic and add 8 peeled and chopped ripe tomatoes (about 2 lb), a pinch of salt, and 1 tablespoon of sugar. Cook over low heat for 45–60 minutes, stirring frequently, until the liquid has evaporated and the sauce has thickened. Stir in ½ teaspoon of ground cinnamon and 1 tablespoon of honey and season generously with black pepper. Cook for another minute and serve hot with the kebabs.

calf's liver kebabs

Serves **6**

Preparation time **15 minutes**, plus resting

Cooking time **8 minutes**

2 lb **calf's liver**, thickly sliced

5 oz **beef caul fat** or **bacon slices**

1 teaspoon **ground cumin**

1 tablespoon **paprika**

¼ teaspoon **black pepper**

salt

french fries, to serve

Broil the liver slices quickly on both sides.

Cut the liver and caul fat into pieces and put in a bowl with the spices and salt. Cover with plastic wrap and place in the refrigerator for 1 hour.

Thread the liver onto 6 skewers, alternating with two pieces of fat on each skewer, and cook for 8 minutes, turning regularly, over hot coals or under a preheated hot broiler.

Serve with french fries.

For carrot & spinach salad to serve as an accompaniment, heat 1 tablespoon of olive oil in a saucepan, then add 6 diagonally sliced carrots, the juice of 2 lemons, 4 teaspoons of sugar, and a large pinch of salt. Cover and cook over low heat until the carrots are just tender, adding a little water, if necessary. Meanwhile, steam 1 (8 oz) package of fresh spinach until just wilted, then drain thoroughly and coarsely chop. Toss the carrots and spinach in a dressing of 1 tablespoon of olive oil, 4 teaspoons of orange juice, ½ teaspoon of sugar, ½ teaspoon of ground cumin, and 2 chopped garlic cloves. Serve warm.

meatball kebabs

Serves **6**
Preparation time **25 minutes**
Cooking time **3 minutes**

1 large **onion**
1 bunch of **flat-leaf parsley**
1 bunch of **cilantro**
1 **mint stem**
2 lb **ground beef**
1 tablespoon **paprika**
1 teaspoon **ground cumin**
pinch of **ras-el-hanout**
salt
chopped **salad vegetables**,
   to serve

Finely mince the onion and herbs together. Transfer to a bowl with the beef, spices, and salt to taste and mix thoroughly.

Form into 24 balls, each about 1½ inches across, then flatten slightly and thread onto 6 skewers, four to a skewer. (You can also flatten them completely to form small burgers.)

Cook for 5 minutes, turning regularly, over hot coals or under a preheated hot broiler.

Serve with a chopped, mixed salad.

For moroccan taktouka-style cooked salad to serve as an accompaniment, cut 3 large, ripe tomatoes into chunks and place them in a saucepan with 2 chopped onions, ½ a cucumber halved lengthwise, seeded, and sliced, and 1 green bell pepper and 1 red bell pepper, seeded and chopped. Add ⅓ cup of boiling water and simmer over low heat for 5 minutes to soften the vegetables. Cool and drain, then toss very gently in a dressing made from the juice of 1 lemon, 3 tablespoons of olive oil, 2 crushed garlic cloves, 2 tablespoons of chopped cilantro, and salt and black pepper to taste.

lamb kebabs

Serves **6**

Preparation time **15 minutes**, plus resting

Cooking time **5 minutes**

2 lb boned **leg of lamb**, cubed
1 **onion**, coarsely chopped
1 bunch of **flat-leaf parsley**, snipped
1 teaspoon **ground cumin**
1 tablespoon **paprika**
¼ teaspoon **black pepper**
salt
3 **flatbreads**, cut in half, to serve

Mix together all the ingredients in a bowl, season with salt, then cover with plastic wrap and place in the refrigerator for 2 hours.

Thread the lamb onto 6 skewers and cook for 5 minutes, turning regularly, over hot coals or under a preheated hot broiler.

Open out the flatbread halves, insert the meat pieces, and serve.

For homemade flatbreads, stir ½ teaspoon of dry yeast into 1 cup warm water. Place 4 cups all-purpose flour in a large bowl, make a well in the center, and pour in ¼ cup of olive oil and the yeast mixture. Using your hands, work the flour into the liquid to make a dough. Knead until smooth and elastic, then set aside in a warm place for 1½ hours. Turn out the dough and divide it into 6 pieces. Roll each piece out thinly, sprinkle with sea salt flakes, and cook on lightly oiled baking sheets in a preheated oven, at 425°F, for about 8 minutes, or until golden.

beef & bell pepper kebabs

Serves **4**

Preparation time **15 minutes**, plus marinating

Cooking time **15 minutes**

1 lb **top sirloin steak**

1 **red bell pepper**, cored and seeded

1 **green bell pepper**, cored and seeded

1 teaspoon crushed **coriander seeds**

3 tablespoons **vegetable oil**

¼ cup chopped **cilantro**

1 **red chile**, seeded and chopped

1 **garlic clove**, crushed

2 tablespoons **lime juice**

4 **chapattis**

salt and **black pepper**

Presoak 8 wooden skewers in warm water. Cut the beef and bell peppers into 1 inch cubes.

Mix together the coriander seeds, 2 tablespoons of oil, and half the chopped cilantro in a bowl and season to taste. Add the beef and bell peppers and toss to coat.

Thread the beef and bell peppers onto the skewers, cover, and refrigerate for up to 1 hour.

Mix together the remaining cilantro and oil with the chile, garlic, and lime juice to make a dressing, season to taste, and set aside.

Broil the skewers under a preheated hot broiler for 15 minutes, turning often and basting with the juices. Warm the chapattis under the broiler.

Serve 2 skewers per person on a hot chapatti and drizzle over the cilantro dressing.

For moroccan lettuce salad to serve as an accompaniment, shred the outer leaves of 2 romaine lettuce hearts and separate the smaller inner leaves. Place the shredded lettuce and whole leaves in a bowl and add 1 finely sliced red onion. Pour the juice of 1 lemon and 2 tablespoons of olive oil over the salad, season generously with sea salt and black pepper, and toss the salad thoroughly.

marinated minty lamb kebabs

Serves **4**

Preparation time **15 minutes**,
  plus marinating

Cooking time **10 minutes**

1 **garlic clove**, crushed

2 tablespoons chopped **mint**

1 tablespoon prepared
  mint sauce

⅔ cup **plain yogurt**

12 oz lean **lamb**, cubed

2 small **onions**, cut into
  wedges

1 **green bell pepper**, cored,
  seeded, and cut into wedges

lemon wedges, green salad,
  and couscous, to serve

Mix together the garlic, mint, mint sauce, and yogurt in a medium bowl, add the lamb, and stir well. Cover and let marinate in a cool place for 10 minutes.

Thread the lamb and onion and bell pepper wedges onto 8 metal skewers and cook under a preheated hot broiler for 8—10 minutes or until cooked through.

Serve the kebabs with lemon wedges and, if desired, accompany them with a green salad and couscous.

For spicy lamb kebabs with ginger, marinate the lamb in a mixture of 2 inches fresh ginger root, peeled and finely grated, ¼ cup each of soy sauce and dry sherry, 1 teaspoon of sugar, and 1 tablespoon of lemon juice. Broil as above.

chicken skewers with couscous

Serves **4**

Preparation time **25 minutes**,
  plus chilling

Cooking time **20–25 minutes**

1 lb boneless, skinless
  chicken breasts
2 tablespoons **olive oil**
2 **garlic cloves**, crushed
½ teaspoon each **ground
  cumin, turmeric, and paprika**
2 teaspoons **lemon juice**

Couscous
¼ cup **olive oil**
1 small **onion**, finely chopped
1 **garlic clove**, crushed
1 teaspoon each **ground cumin,
  cinnamon, black pepper**, and
  ginger
⅓ cup each **dried dates, dried
  apricots, and** blanched
  almonds, toasted
2½ cups **vegetable stock**,
  boiling
1 cup **couscous**
1 tablespoon **lemon juice**
2 tablespoons chopped **cilantro**
salt and **black pepper**
pomegranate seeds, lemon
  wedges, and **cilantro** sprigs,
  to garnish

Cut the chicken into long thin strips, place in a shallow dish, and add the olive oil, garlic, spices, and lemon juice. Stir well, cover, and let marinate for 2 hours. Thread the chicken strips onto 8 presoaked wooden skewers.

Prepare the couscous by heating half the oil in a saucepan and sautéing the onion, garlic, and spices for 5 minutes. Chop and stir in the dried fruits and almonds and remove from the heat.

Meanwhile, put the couscous in a heatproof bowl, add a boiling stock, cover with a dish towel, and steam for 8–10 minutes, or acording to the package directions, until all the liquid is absorbed. Stir in the remaining oil and the fruit-and-nut mixture, add the lemon juice and cilantro, and season to taste.

While the couscous is steaming, broil the chicken skewers for 4–5 minutes on each side, until charred and cooked through. Serve with the couscous, garnished with pomegranate seeds, lemon wedges, and cilantro, if desired.

For roasted chicken with herb couscous, mix the oil, garlic, spices, and lemon juice and drizzle over 8 skinned and slashed chicken thighs. Roast in a preheated oven, at 375°F, for 35–45 minutes. Steam the couscous as above in stock. Stir in the remaining oil and lemon juice. Add 4 finely chopped scallions, 3 tablespoons of chopped mint, 3 tablespoons of chopped parsley, and 2 chopped tomatoes. Spoon onto plates, top with the chicken, and serve with lemon wedges.

vegetables

potatoes "mchermel"

Serves **6**
Preparation time **15 minutes**
Cooking time **20 minutes**

8 **white round potatoes**
   (about 2 lb)
1 bunch of **flat-leaf parsley**
1 bunch of **cilantro**
3 **garlic cloves**
3 tablespoons **olive oil**
1 tablespoon **paprika**
½ teaspoon **ground cumin**
pinch of **cayenne pepper**
1¼ cups **water**
salt

Peel and wash the potatoes, then cut into medium-size pieces. Chop the herbs and garlic together.

Heat the oil in a heavy flameproof casserole. Add the chopped herbs and garlic, cook for 2 minutes, then add the potatoes.

Cook for 3 minutes, add the spices and salt to taste, then pour in the water. Cover the dish, lower the heat, and cook for 15 minutes, until the sauce has reduced.

For potatoes with fennel, place 3 tablespoons of olive oil in a saucepan with 1¼ lb halved new potatoes. Place 3 trimmed and quartered fennel bulbs on top with 3 sliced garlic cloves. Season to taste with salt and black pepper, then cover with water, bring to a boil, and simmer, covered, for 15 minutes. Add ¼ cup each of chopped mint and basil, then cook, uncovered, for another 10 minutes, until the vegetables are tender and the sauce is reduced. Stir in 2 tablespoons of lemon juice and serve drizzled with olive oil.

green lentils in tomato sauce

Serves **6**
Preparation time **15 minutes**
Cooking time **25 minutes**

3 tablespoons **olive oil**
1 **onion**, chopped
2 **garlic cloves**, chopped
3 **tomatoes**, skinned and
   crushed
1 cup **water**
½ teaspoon **tomato paste**
2½ cups **green lentils**
½ teaspoon **paprika**
1 **red bell pepper**, cored,
   seeded, and coarsely
   chopped
1 bunch **flat-leaf parsley**
salt and **bell pepper**

Heat the oil in a heavy flameproof casserole, add the onion, garlic, and tomatoes, and cook for 10 minutes.

Add the water, stir in the tomato paste, then add the lentils, paprika, and salt and pepper to taste.

Add the bell pepper and the parsley to the dish and continue to cook over low heat for 10 minutes, until the sauce has reduced.

For lentils with cumin, heat 2 tablespoons of oil and gently sauté 2 sliced onions and 4 chopped garlic cloves until softened. Stir in 2½ cups green lentils, 4 teaspoons of crushed cumin seeds, and 2 teaspoons of crushed coriander seeds. Pour 1 cup of water over the lentils and cook over low heat for 20–25 minutes, until the lentils are tender. Stir in 1 tablespoon of lemon juice and season to taste with salt and black pepper.

saffron-scented vegetable tagine

Serves **4**
Preparation time **15 minutes**
Cooking time **50 minutes**

½ cup **sunflower oil**
1 large **onion**, finely chopped
2 **garlic cloves**, crushed
2 teaspoons each **ground coriander**, **cumin**, and **cinnamon**
1 (15 oz) can **chickpeas**, drained
1 (14½ oz) can **diced tomatoes**
2½ cups **vegetable stock**
¼ teaspoon **saffron threads**
1 large **eggplant**, trimmed and chopped
8 oz **white button mushrooms**, trimmed and halved if large
½ cup chopped **dried figs**
2 tablespoons chopped fresh **cilantro**
salt and **black pepper**
steamed **couscous**, to serve

Heat 2 tablespoons of the oil in a skillet, add the onion, garlic, and spices, and cook over medium heat, stirring frequently, for 5 minutes, until golden. Using a slotted spoon, transfer to a saucepan and add the chickpeas, tomatoes, stock, and saffron. Season with salt and pepper.

Heat the remaining oil in the skillet, add the eggplant, and cook over high heat, stirring frequently, for 5 minutes, until browned. Add to the stew and bring to a boil, then reduce the heat, cover, and simmer gently for 20 minutes.

Stir in the mushrooms and figs and simmer gently, uncovered, for another 20 minutes. Stir in the fresh cilantro and adjust the seasoning. Serve with steamed couscous.

For winter vegetable & lentil tagine, replace the eggplant with 2 sliced carrots and 2 cubed potatoes. Instead of the chickpeas, use a drained (15 oz) can of green lentils or 2 cups of cooked dried lentils (⅔ cup when uncooked). Follow the recipe above and stir in ½ cup chopped dried apricots instead of the figs.

zucchini with tomatoes

Serves **6**
Preparation time **10 minutes**
Cooking time **20 minutes**

3 tablespoons **olive oil**
1 **onion**, finely sliced
3 **tomatoes**, diced
3 **garlic cloves**
1 tablespoon **paprika**
1 cup **water**
5 **zucchini** (about 2 lb),
   trimmed and cut into circles,
   then halved or quartered
salt

Heat the oil in a heavy flameproof casserole, add the onion and tomatoes, and soften for 5 minutes. Add the garlic, paprika, and salt to taste and pour in the water.

When the sauce is simmering, add the zucchini and cook for 15 minutes.

Remove from the heat once the sauce has reduced.

For okra with tomatoes, heat ¼ cup of olive oil and sauté 3 thinly sliced onions with 3 teaspoons of crushed coriander seeds for about 4 minutes, until starting to brown. Add 1½ lb whole okra, trimmed, and 4 crushed garlic cloves and cook for another 1 minute. Stir in 6 peeled and chopped tomatoes (about 1½ lb) and 1 teaspoon of sugar and simmer over low heat, stirring occasionally, until the okra is tender and the sauce has reduced. Stir in 2 teaspoons of finely grated lemon rind and 3 tablespoons of lemon juice, and season to taste with salt and black pepper.

white navy beans in tomato sauce

Serves **6**
Preparation time **10 minutes**
Cooking time **30 minutes**

2 **tomatoes**, skinned
1 small **onion**
2 **garlic cloves**
3 tablespoons **olive oil**
1 cup **water**
1 (15 oz) can **white navy beans**, rinsed and drained
½ **lemon**, juiced
½ bunch of **flat-leaf parsley**, snipped
½ bunch of **cilantro**, snipped
½ teaspoon **sweet paprika**
½ teaspoon **ground ginger**
¼ teaspoon **ground turmeric**
salt

Blend the tomatoes, onion, and garlic. Heat the oil in a heavy flameproof casserole, add the blended vegetables, and cook gently for 10 minutes, until the mixture has reduced. Pour in the water, let return to a simmer, then add the beans.

Simmer for 15 minutes, then add the lemon juice, herbs, and spices. Season lightly with salt. Let sit over gentle heat for another 5 minutes, then serve warm.

For chickpeas in tomato sauce, sauté 1 large sliced onion, 2 crushed garlic cloves, 4 chopped dried apricots, 1½ teaspoons of ras-el-hanout, ½ a cinnamon stick, a pinch of dried red pepper flakes, and salt and black pepper to taste in 3 tablespoons of olive oil for 7–8 minutes, stirring occasionally, to soften the onion. Add 2 (15 oz) cans of chickpeas, rinsed and drained, and 1 (14½ oz) can of diced tomatoes. Bring to a boil and simmer for 5 minutes, until the sauce has reduced. Add the finely grated rind and juice of ½ a lemon, ¼ cup of chopped cilantro, and 1 tablespoon of chopped mint. Cook for another 5 minutes, then serve warm.

bissara (split pea dip)

Serves **6**
Preparation time **10 minutes**
Cooking time **20 minutes**

Dip
2½ cups **split peas**
1 **turnip**, peeled and chopped
2 **garlic cloves**
pinch of **salt**

To serve
1 **lemon**, juiced
6 pinches of **ground cumin**
6 pinches of **sweet paprika**
3 teaspoons **olive oil**
warm crusty **bread**

Put the ingredients into a heavy flameproof casserole with a pinch of salt. Cover with water, then bring to a boil, cover the dish, and simmer over low heat for 50 minutes or until the peas are tender, adding more boiling water, if necessary, during cooking.

Put in a blender or rub through a food-mill to create a smooth puree.

Serve in individual dishes with a few drops of lemon juice, a pinch of spices, and a little olive oil, accompanied by some warm crusty bread.

For fava bean bissara, place 3⅓ cups soaked and drained dried fava beans in a saucepan with 4 garlic cloves and 2 teaspoons of cumin seeds. Cover with water, then bring to a boil, cover the pan, and simmer over low heat for about 1 hour or until the beans are tender, adding more boiling water, if necessary, during cooking. Drain the beans, reserving the liquid, and place in a food processor with ⅔ cup olive oil, the juice of 3 lemons, ¼ cup of the reserved cooking liquid, and 1 teaspoon each of paprika and cayenne pepper. Process to a smooth, thin puree, adding a little more of the reserved cooking liquid, if necessary. Season with salt to taste and serve warm, drizzled with extra olive oil.

couscous

grilled vegetables & couscous

Serves **4**
Preparation time **20 minutes**
Cooking time **16–20 minutes**

1 large **eggplant**
2 large **zucchini**
2 **red bell peppers**, cored,
   seeded and quartered
¼ cup **olive oil**
1 cup **couscous**
2 cups boiling **vegetable
   stock**
4 tablespoons **butter**
2 tablespoons chopped
   mixed herbs, such as mint,
   cilantro, and parsley
1 **lemon,** juiced
salt and **black pepper**

Tahini yogurt sauce
½ cup **Greek-style yogurt**
1 tablespoon **tahini paste**
1 **garlic clove**, crushed
½ tablespoon **lemon juice**
1 tablespoon **extra-virgin
   olive oil**

Cut the eggplant and zucchini into ¼ inch thick slices and put in a large bowl with the red bell peppers. Add the olive oil and salt and pepper and stir well.

Heat a ridged grill pan until hot. Add the vegetables, in batches, and cook for 3–4 minutes on each side, depending on size, until charred and tender.

Meanwhile, prepare the couscous. Put the couscous in a heatproof bowl. Pour over the boiling stock, cover, and let soak for 5 minutes. Fluff up the grains with a fork and stir in the butter, herbs, lemon juice, and salt and pepper to taste.

Make the tahini yogurt sauce by combining all the ingredients in a bowl and season with salt and pepper. Serve with the vegetables and couscous.

For garlic mayonnaise to serve instead of the tahini yogurt sauce, crush 1–2 garlic cloves and stir into ⅔ cup good-quality mayonnaise. Serve with the vegetables and couscous.

couscous with raisins & chickpeas

Serves **6**

Preparation time **15 minutes**

Cooking time **30 minutes**

6 tablespoons **butter**

¼ cup **olive oil**

3 lb boned **shoulder of lamb**, cubed

4 **onions**, finely chopped

1 cup **chickpeas** (rinsed and drained if using canned or soaked overnight if using dried)

½ teaspoon **ground ginger**

½ teaspoon **ground turmeric**

pinch of **saffron**

½ teaspoon **black pepper**

½ teaspoon **salt**

4 cups **water**

2¾ cups **raisins**

2½ cups medium-grain **couscous**

Heat half the butter and the oil in a heavy flameproof casserole or a couscous steamer. Add the meat and onion. When the meat is browned on all sides, add the chickpeas, spices, and salt.

Pour in the water, cover, and let cook for 20 minutes. Add the raisins and cook for another 5 minutes.

Meanwhile, prepare the couscous following the method on pages 12–13.

Transfer the couscous to a large, shallow serving dish, arrange the meat in the center, and top with the broth, raisins, and chickpeas.

For vegetable & chickpea couscous, soften a finely chopped onion and 2 crushed garlic cloves in 3 tablespoons of olive oil. Add 1 tablespoon of tomato paste, ½ teaspoon each of cayenne pepper and turmeric, and 1 teaspoon each of ground coriander and cumin, and cook, stirring, for 2 minutes. Stir in 2 cups of cauliflower florets, a diced red pepper, and 1 cup of water. Bring to a boil, then simmer for 10 minutes. Add 4 peeled and chopped ripe tomatoes, 2 sliced zucchini, and 1 (15 oz) can of chickpeas, rinsed and drained. Cook for another 10 minutes. Season to taste and serve with the couscous, garnished with cilantro sprigs.

chicken couscous salad

Serves **4**
Preparation time **20 minutes**,
  plus marinating
Cooking time **20 minutes**

4 boneless, skinless **chicken
  breasts**, about 4 oz each
1 ½ cups **couscous**
1 ¼ cups hot **chicken stock**
1 **pomegranate**
rind and juice of 1 **orange**
small bunch of **cilantro**
small bunch of **mint**

Marinade
1 ½ tablespoons **curry paste**
  (tikka masala)
⅓ cup **plain yogurt**
1 teaspoon **olive oil**
2 tablespoons **lemon juice**

Make the marinade by mixing the curry paste, yogurt, and oil. Put the chicken in a nonmetallic dish, cover with half the marinade, and let sit for at least 1 hour.

Put the couscous in a bowl, add the hot stock, cover, and let sit for 8 minutes.

Meanwhile, cut the pomegranate in half and remove the seeds. Add them to the couscous with the orange rind and juice.

Remove the chicken from the marinade, reserving the marinade, and transfer to an aluminum foil-lined baking sheet. Cook in a preheated oven, at 375°F, for 6—7 minutes, then transfer to a preheated hot broiler and cook for 2 minutes, until caramelized. Cover with foil and let rest for 5 minutes.

Chop the cilantro and mint coarsely, reserving some whole cilantro leaves for garnish, and add to the couscous. Thinly slice the chicken. Spoon the couscous onto plates and add the chicken. Thin the reserved marinade with the lemon juice and drizzle it over the couscous. Garnish with the reserved cilantro leaves and serve immediately.

For pomegranate vinaigrette, an alternative dressing for this salad, whisk together ⅔ cup pomegranate juice, 2 tablespoons pomegranate molasses (available from Middle Eastern stores), 2 tablespoons red wine vinegar, and 3 tablespoons olive oil.

sweet couscous with raisins

Serves **6**
Preparation time **20 minutes**
Cooking time **30 minutes**

1¼ sticks **butter**
2 tablespoons **olive oil**
4 **onions**, finely chopped
3½ lb **chicken**, cut into pieces
1 **cinnamon stick**
½ teaspoon **ground ginger**
½ teaspoon **ground turmeric**
pinch of **saffron**
½ teaspoon **black pepper**
1 tablespoon **salt**
3½ cups **raisins**
2 tablespoons **sugar**
2 tablespoons **honey**
1 tablespoon **ground
  cinnamon**
2½ cups medium-grain
  couscous

Heat two-thirds of the butter and the oil in a heavy flameproof casserole or a couscous steamer. Add the onions and let soften.

Add the chicken pieces, cinnamon stick, spices, and salt. Pour in enough water to cover and let cook for 20 minutes. Remove the onions with a slotted spoon.

Put 2 ladlefuls of the broth in a small saucepan with the raisins, sugar, honey, and ground cinnamon. Simmer for 5 minutes.

Meanwhile, prepare the couscous following the method on pages 12–13.

Arrange the chicken pieces in a serving dish, surround with the couscous, and top with the spicy raisins.

For sweet vegetable couscous, gently sauté 1 sliced red onion, 1 crushed garlic clove, and 1 chopped red chile in 2 tablespoons of olive oil for 5 minutes, then stir in ½ teaspoon each of ground ginger and cinnamon and cook for another 2 minutes. Add 1 (14½ oz) can of diced tomatoes, 4 sliced carrots, 2 cubed turnips, ⅓ cup raisins, and 1 cup vegetable stock and simmer for 20 minutes, or until the vegetables are tender. Add 2 sliced zucchini, 1 (15 oz) can of chickpeas, rinsed and drained, 2 tablespoons of honey, and 3 tablespoons each of chopped flat-leaf parsley and cilantro, and cook for another 10 minutes. Serve with couscous.

sweet & salty couscous "medfouna"

Serves **6**
Preparation time **20 minutes**
Cooking time **25 minutes**

6 tablespoons **butter**
2 tablespoons **sunflower oil**
2 **onions**, finely chopped
2 small **chickens**, cut into
  pieces
1 bunch of **cilantro**, chopped
1/4 teaspoon **ground ginger**
1/2 teaspoon **ground turmeric**
pinch of **saffron**
1/4 teaspoon **black pepper**
1/2 cup **water**
2 1/2 cups medium-grain
  couscous
salt
1 tablespoon **cinnamon**,
  to garnish
**superfine sugar or
  confectioners' sugar**,
  to serve

Melt half the butter and the oil in a heavy flameproof casserole and soften the onion for 2 minutes.

Add the chicken pieces with the chopped cilantro, spices, salt to taste, and water. Cook for 20 minutes, stirring from time to time.

When the meat is tender, remove the casserole from the heat, strip the meat from the bones, and mix well with the sauce.

Meanwhile, prepare the couscous following the method on pages 12–13.

Place one-third of the couscous on a large serving dish. Spread with half the chicken mixture, then cover with another third of the couscous. Spread with the remaining chicken mixture and top with the remaining couscous.

Garnish with the cinnamon and serve with the sugar.

For quick fruit couscous to serve as an accompaniment to meat dishes, bring 2 cups chicken or vegetable stock to a boil, then add 4 tablespoons of unsalted butter and 1/3 cup each of chopped dried dates, chopped dried apricots, and golden raisins. Boil for 3 minutes, then remove from the heat and add 2 1/2 cups couscous. Cover and set aside for 5 minutes, then stir in 2–3 teaspoons of cinnamon, and 1/2 cup toasted slivered almonds.

couscous with buttermilk

Serves **6**

Preparation time **5 minutes**

Cooking time **10 minutes**

2½ cups medium-grain
couscous

3¼ cups frozen **fava beans**

8 cups **buttermilk**

pinch of **salt**

Prepare the couscous following the method on pages 12–13.

Meanwhile, cook the fava beans in boiling salted water for 10 minutes.

Separate the couscous grains with your hands, then fill 6 serving bowls halfway with the couscous and pour the buttermilk over it. Serve the fava beans separately.

For couscous with yogurt dressing, prepare the couscous and cook the fava beans as above. Place the couscous in a serving bowl with most of the fava beans. Gently fold in a dressing made from 1 cup Greek yogurt, ⅓ cup of water, the finely grated rind and juice of ½ a lemon, 3 tablespoons of chopped cilantro, 1 garlic clove crushed with salt, and 2 teaspoons of crushed toasted cumin seeds. Serve garnished with the remaining fava beans and some cilantro sprigs.

couscous with cinnamon & milk

Serves **6**
Preparation time **5 minutes**
Cooking time **10 minutes**

2½ cups fine-grain **couscous**
1¼ sticks **butter**
1 tablespoon **peanut oil**
1 tablespoon **cinnamon**, to
  garnish
1 tablespoon **sugar**,
  plus extra to serve
4 cups **milk**, to accompany

Prepare the couscous following the method on pages 12–13, but incorporating the 1¼ sticks of butter.

Arrange on a serving dish in a cone shape, garnished with the cinnamon and sugar. Serve with milk and extra sugar, to taste.

For couscous with fruit & nuts, before shaping the couscous into a cone, stir through ⅓ cup of fruit and ½ cup of nuts in one of the following combinations: raisins and toasted blanched almonds; golden raisins and unsalted pistachios; or fresh chopped dates and chopped walnuts.

pastillas

chicken pastilla

Serves **8**
Preparation time **30 minutes**
Cooking time **45 minutes**

9 **onions** (about 3 lb)
2 bunches of **flat-leaf parsley**
1¾ sticks **butter**
2 tablespoons **sunflower oil**
3½ lb **chicken**, cut into 8 pieces
½ teaspoon **ground turmeric**
pinch of **saffron**
½ teaspoon **salt**
½ teaspoon **black pepper**
12 **eggs**
1 **lemon**, juiced
1 pack of **phyllo pastry**
3 tablespoons **all-purpose flour** plus 2 tablespoons **water**, to seal

Finely mince the onions and parsley. Heat the butter and oil in a heavy saucepan and add the onions, parsley, chicken, spices, and half the salt and black pepper. When the chicken is cooked, remove the skin and bones and reserve the meat.

Beat the eggs with the remaining salt and black pepper and pour into the cooking juices in the pan. Stir rapidly with a wooden spatula and cook until they set. Transfer to a plate and let cool. Stir in the lemon juice.

Prepare the pastilla as shown on pages 14–15. Spread the cooled eggs in a thick layer over the bottom and place the chicken meat on top. Cover with the phyllo sheets, seal, and butter as described. Bake in a preheated oven, at 350°F, for 30 minutes. Serve hot.

For vegetable pastilla, toss 1 chopped butternut squash and 8 oz quartered shallots in ¼ cup of olive oil mixed with 1 teaspoon each of crushed, toasted cumin and coriander seeds, 1 teaspoon each of ground cumin and paprika, ½ teaspoon of ground cinnamon, and salt to taste. Cook in a preheated oven, at 350°F, for 20–25 minutes, until golden. Meanwhile, sauté 1 cup each of blanched almonds and pistachios with 2 teaspoons of grated ginger root in 1 tablespoon of olive oil until golden, then add ½ cup of golden raisins. Stir in 1 (8 oz) package fresh young spinach and cook until wilted. Add 2 tablespoons of honey, then combine with the roasted vegetables. Complete the pastilla following the steps shown on pages 14–15.

pigeon pastilla

Serves **8**

Preparation time **40 minutes**

Cooking time **45 minutes**

Pastilla

3 large **onions**

2 bunches **flat-leaf parsley**

½ bunch **cilantro**

1¾ sticks **butter**

3 tablespoons **sunflower oil**

7 **pigeons**, quartered

½ teaspoon **salt**

½ teaspoon **black pepper**

1 teaspoon **ground cinnamon**

1 cup **water**

12 **eggs**

pinch of **saffron**

¼ teaspoon **turmeric**

1¾ cups blanched **almonds**

½ cup **superfine sugar** or **granulated sugar**

1 packageof **phyllo pastry**

3 tablespoons **all-purpose flour** plus 2 tablespoons **water**, to seal

¾ cup **confectioners' sugar** plus 1 tablespoon **cinnamon**, to garnish

Finely mince the onions and herbs. Heat the butter and sunflower oil in a heavy saucepan and add the pigeons, onions, herbs, salt, black pepper, and half the cinnamon. Mix well. Add the water, cover, and cook for 15 minutes. Transfer the pigeon pieces to a plate and remove the white meat from the bones (keep the thighs whole).

Beat the eggs with a little salt and black pepper, the saffron, and turmeric and pour into the cooking juices in the pan. Stir rapidly with a wooden spatula and cook until they set. Transfer to a plate and let cool.

Dry-toast the almonds in a skillet, then set aside to cool. Once they are cool, crush and mix with the sugar and the remaining cinnamon and set aside.

Prepare the pastilla following the steps on pages 14–15. Spread the cooled eggs in a thick layer over the bottom and place the pigeon meat on top. Generously sprinkle with the almond-and-cinnamon mixture. Cover with the phyllo sheets, seal, and butter as described. Bake in a preheated oven, at 350°F, for 30 minutes.

To serve, sprinkle the top of the pastilla with the confectioners' sugar and use the cinnamon to form intersecting lines.

For pigeon pastilla with ginger, add a 3 inch piece of grated fresh ginger root and use a cinnamon stick instead of cinnamon in the first step. Reduce the quantity of turmeric added to the beaten eggs to a large pinch.

fish & shrimp pastilla

Serves **8**
Preparation time **15 minutes**,
  plus marinating time
Cooking time **45 minutes**

2 lb **white fish fillets**
1 lb **shrimp**, shelled and
  deveined
1 bunch of **cilantro**, chopped
1 bunch of **flat-leaf parsley**,
  chopped
3 **garlic cloves**, finely minced
1 tablespoon **paprika**
pinch of **cayenne pepper**
½ teaspoon **ground cumin**
pinch of **mace**
¼ teaspoon **salt**
¼ teaspoon **black pepper**
2 tablespoons **white wine
  vinegar**
4 tablespoons **butter**
2 tablespoons **olive oil**
1 large bowl of fine **Chinese
  noodles**, soaked according
  to the package directions
1 package of **phyllo pastry**
3 tablespoons **all-purpose
  flour** plus 2 tablespoons
  water, to seal

Put the fish and shrimp in a large bowl with the herbs, garlic, spices, salt and black pepper, and vinegar. Cover with plastic wrap and refrigerate for 1 hour.

Melt the butter in a heavy flameproof casserole, add the oil, and cook the fish and shrimp until the flesh begins to flake. Stir in the soaked noodles and cook for 10 minutes over low heat.

Preheat the oven to 350°F.

Prepare the pastilla following the steps on pages 14–15. Spread the filling in a thick layer over the bottom. Cover with the phyllo sheets, seal, and butter as described.

Transfer to the oven and bake for 30 minutes.

For fish pastilla with squid, replace 1 lb of the white fish fillets with 1 lb squid, cleaned and cut into large pieces. Remove the squid pieces from the marinade, cut them into smaller pieces, and quickly cook them in the butter and oil until just opaque, then remove from the casserole and set aside while you cook the white fish and shrimp. Return to the dish with the soaked noodles and complete the recipe as above.

pastilla with custard

Serves **8**

Preparation time **30 minutes**

Cooking time **20 minutes**

Pastilla

1¾ cups blanched **almonds**

¼ cup **superfine sugar**

20 sheets of **phyllo pastry**

sunflower oil, for frying

Custard

4 **egg yolks**

¾ cup **superfine sugar** or **granulated sugar**

1 tablespoon **vanilla sugar**

2 tablespoons **all-purpose flour**

3 cups boiling **milk**

To decorate

4 **egg whites**

¾ cup **superfine sugar** or **granulated sugar**

1 tablespoon **water**

Dry-toast the almonds, then set aside to cool. Once cold, coarsely chop and mix with the superfine sugar.

Put the egg yolks for the custard in a saucepan with the sugars and beat to dissolve. Incorporate the flour, then pour in a boiling milk, beating vigorously over low heat until the custard thickens. Let cool.

Beat the egg whites with ¼ cup of the superfine sugar until stiff. Cook spoonfuls of the meringue mixture in boiling water and set aside.

Fold the phyllo pastry sheets in four, fan fashion, and cook them in the sunflower oil, a few at a time, then drain on paper towels. Place four of the pastry fans on a round plate to form a circle, then add a second layer. Spread with half the cold custard and sprinkle over one-third of the almonds. Repeat to make another layer, then top with the remaining four fans.

Decorate with the meringue and sprinkle with the remaining almonds. Quickly prepare a sauce with the remaining superfine sugar and the tablespoon of water. Drizzle it over the pastilla and serve immediately.

For "ktefa," prepare the recipe as above, omitting the meringues and sauce and adding 2 teaspoons of orange-flower water to the custard before letting it cool. Spread each of the first two layers of pastry fans with one-third of the custard, then spread the remaining third on the top layer of pastry fans. Sprinkle with almonds and ground cinnamon before serving.

desserts &
sweet things

orange salad

Serves **6**
Preparation time **10 minutes**

8 **oranges**
1 tablespoon **confectioners'
  sugar**
¼ teaspoon **cinnamon**
⅓ cup blanched **almonds**,
  to decorate

Peel 7 of the oranges, removing most of the white pith with the rind. Cut them into ½ inch thick circles and arrange on a serving plate.

Sprinkle with sugar and squeeze the juice of the remaining orange over the circles.

Sprinkle with cinnamon and decorate with the almonds.

For mixed fruit salad, mix the juice of 2 oranges with 3 tablespoons of honey and 1½ teaspoons of orange-flower water in a serving bowl. Add 1½ cups each of chopped nectarines, apricots, and mangoes, stirring the fruit into the orange-and-honey dressing as you add it to prevent discoloration. Marinate for 1 hour and serve at room temperature, sprinkled with pomegranate seeds and fresh mint sprigs.

squash preserves

Preparation time **15 minutes**
Cooking time **20 minutes**

1 large **butternut squash** or
  kabocha squash, peeled,
  seeded, and diced
3¾ cups **superfine sugar** or
  granulated sugar
1 **lemon**, juiced
1 tablespoon **cinnamon**

Drop the diced squash into boiling water and cook for 5 minutes.

Drain the squash. Put into a large saucepan, sprinkle with the sugar, and pour in the lemon juice. Cook over low heat for 15 minutes, gently stirring from time to time.

Stir in the cinnamon at the end of cooking. Store in sterilized jars in the refrigerator and use within a month.

For pumpkin pastilla, blanch 8 cups peeled pumpkin or buttenut squash chunks in boiling water for 10 minutes. Drain, then cook in 4 tablespoons of butter over low heat for 30 minutes, stirring occasionally. Mash to a puree, then stir in ¼ cup sugar, 2 tablespoons of honey, a pinch of saffron, ½ teaspoon each of ground ginger and cinnamon, and ¼ teaspoon of salt, and cook, stirring, until the puree is dry and firm. Remove from the heat and stir in 2 cups chopped walnuts. Mix 1¼ cups of confectioners' sugar with 2 cups of toasted slivered almonds, ¼ teaspoon of ground cinnamon, and 2 tablespoons of orange-flower water. Prepare the pastilla (see pages 14–15) and fill with the pumpkin puree topped with the almond mixture. Cook in a preheated oven, at 350°F, for 30 minutes, or until golden. Serve sprinkled with confectioners' sugar and ground cinnamon.

candied oranges

Soaking time **12 hours**
Preparation time **20 minutes**
Cooking time **20 minutes**

3 lb **navel oranges**
5 cups **superfine sugar** or
  granulated sugar
1 **lemon**, juiced
¼ teaspoon **salt**

Select thick-skinned oranges. Grate them to remove the rind, then place the oranges in a bowl of salted water and let soak overnight.

Rinse the oranges under plenty of running water, then bring to a boil in a saucepan of water. As soon as the water boils, remove and drain the oranges. Cut into quarters or sixths, depending on size.

Place the pieces in a large stainless steel saucepan, cover with sugar, pour in the lemon juice, and cook over low heat, gently turning the pieces once to avoid damaging them.

Once the oranges are a rich golden color and the syrup has reduced, remove from the heat and arrange in serving dishes.

For candied lemon peel to serve with coffee, peel 6 thick-skinned, unwaxed lemons in lengthwise quarters. Scrape off most of the white pith. Place the peel in a stainless steel saucepan, cover with cold water, then bring to a boil and blanch for 1 minute. Drain and repeat, then slice the peel into thin strips. Bring 2 cups of water to a boil with 2½ cups of sugar and simmer for 45 minutes. Stir the lemon peel strips into the syrup and simmer for 10 minutes. Let cool in the syrup overnight, then drain. Working in batches, toss the strips in sugar until coated, then spread them out on baking sheets to dry. Store in the refrigerator in a sterilized airtight jar.

eggplant preserves

Soaking time **12 hours**
Preparation time **10 minutes**
Cooking time **45 minutes**

2 lb very small **eggplants**
5 cups **granulated sugar**
1 cup **water**
1 **lemon**, juiced
5 or 6 **cloves**
¼ teaspoon **allspice**
2 small pieces **gum arabic**
salt

Prick the eggplants all over with a fork. Place them in a large bowl of salted water and let soak overnight.

Rinse the eggplants in plenty of running water, then drop into boiling water and cook for 10 minutes. Drain and set aside.

Put the sugar into a large saucepan with the water and let dissolve slowly. Pour in the lemon juice, then add the spices, gum arabic, and the drained eggplants. Once the eggplants have absorbed the sugar, turn off the heat and drain. Store in sterilized jars in the refrigerator and use with a month.

For fresh fig preserves, place 2 lb quartered fresh figs in a saucepan with ¾ cup granulated sugar, 1¼ cups water, and the finely grated rind and juice of 1 lemon. Slowly bring to a boil, then simmer over low heat, stirring occasionally, for about 1½ hours or until the figs are cooked and the preserves is thick. Store in sterilized jars in the refrigerator and use within a month.

golden raisin & walnut preserves

Preparation time **5 minutes**
Cooking time **50 minutes**

7 cups large **golden raisins**
1 cup **superfine sugar**
¼ teaspoon **ground cinnamon**
2 tablespoons **peanut oil**
1 cup **water**
4 cups **walnut pieces**

Rinse the golden raisins and place in a large saucepan with the sugar, cinnamon, oil, and water.

Cook over very low heat for about 45 minutes, stirring from time to time; the golden raisins should not be too colored.

Meanwhile, dry-toast the walnuts over low heat for 5 minutes, then remove and let cool. When they are cold, coarsely crush them in your hand and add them to the golden raisins 5 minutes before the end of cooking.

Put into a sterilized jar and let cool. Store in the refrigerator and use within a month.

For fig & walnut preserves, replace the golden raisins with 3½ cups raisins and 2½ cups chopped dried figs (trim and discard the stems). Replace the cinnamon with 2 teaspoons of ras-el-hanout.

preserved clementines

Soaking time **12 hours**
Preparation time **10 minutes**
Cooking time **2 hours**

14–16 small **clementines**
(about 2 lb)
5 cups **sugar**
1 **lemon**, juiced
4 cups **water**

Place the clementines in a bowl of water and let soak overnight.

Pierce the fruit from top to bottom and on all sides with the tip of a sharp knife.

Place the clementines in a large saucepan, sprinkle with the sugar and lemon juice, and pour in the water. Heat over low heat until the sugar dissolves.

Cook for a total of 2 hours, in three or four stages, letting the fruit cool between each stage.

For clementine cake, process 4 well-drained preserved clementines to a fairly coarse puree in a food processor. Transfer to a mixing bowl and stir in ⅓ cup of sunflower oil, 3 tablespoons of argan oil, 1 cup milk, and ¼ cup honey. Sift together 1¾ cups all-purpose flour with 1½ teaspoons of baking powder, 2 teaspoons of baking soda, and ¼ teaspoon of salt, and fold into the clementine mixture. Pour into a greased and lined cake pan and cook in a preheated oven, at 350°F, for about 45 minutes, or until just firm to the touch.

caramelized nuts

Preparation time **10 minutes**
Cooking time **15 minutes**

1 cup unblanched **almonds**
 or **pistachios**
½ cup **superfine sugar** or
 granulated sugar
1 tablespoon **peanut oil**

Heat a nonstick skillet over very low heat.

Add the almonds or pistachios and sugar and heat, stirring from time to time with a wooden spatula, until the sugar melts and turns to caramel.

Oil a baking sheet with the peanut oil, then use a spoon to remove a few nuts and form into a small pile on the sheet. Repeat with all the nuts.

Once the nuts are cold, transfer from the baking sheet to a serving plate.

For caramelized sesame seeds, add 1 cup of white sesame seeds and 1 cup superfine or granulated sugar to a nonstick skillet over very low heat. Let the sugar melt and caramelize as above. Transfer the mixture into an oiled baking sheet and flatten the surface with a rolling pin. Cut into small pieces while still hot and soft.

almond "ghoriba"

Makes around **30**
Preparation time **20 minutes**
Cooking time **20 minutes**

6¾ cups blanched **almonds**
(about 2 lb) plus a few extra,
to decorate
4 cups **confectioners' sugar**
½ tablespoon **baking powder**
3 tablespoons melted **butter**
6 **egg yolks**
2 **whole eggs**
rind of 1 **lemon**
⅔ cup **orange-flower water**

Preheat the oven to 350°F.

Finely chop the almonds in a blender.

Put the almonds in a mixing bowl and mix in two-thirds of the confectioners' sugar, the baking powder, butter, egg yolks and whole eggs, and lemon rind.

Add the orange-flower water to make a dough. Using wet hands, form into balls about the size of a walnut.

Put the remaining confectioners' sugar onto a plate and roll each ball in it until coated. Place on an oiled baking sheet, spaced well apart. Press an almond into the top of each one and transfer to the oven. Cook for 15 minutes.

For speedy almond "ghoriba," place 6 cups ground almonds (almond meal) in a food processor with 1 cup of superfine or granulated sugar, the finely grated rind of 1½ lemons, 3–4 drops of almond extract, and 2 large egg whites. Process to a soft paste. Using wet hands, form into balls about the size of a walnut. Roll each ball in confectioners' sugar, as above, then place on a greased baking sheet, flattening the balls slightly. Press a blanched almond into the top of each one. Bake in a preheated oven, at 400°F, for 15 minutes.

date crescents

Makes around **40**
Preparation time **30 minutes**
Cooking time **15 minutes**

Pastry dough
4 cups **all-purpose flour**
pinch of **baking powder**
²/₃ cup **granulated sugar**
2 sticks **butter**, melted

Filling
8 oz of **date paste** (or use
  1¾ cups pitted, chopped
  dates)
1 pat of **butter**
½ teaspoon **cinnamon**
1 cup **confectioners' sugar**

Preheat the oven to 300°F.

Make the pastry by mixing all the ingredients to form a dough. Let stand to rest while you make the filling.

Mix all the ingredients for the filling and form into balls the size of a hazelnut.

Form the dough into balls the size of a walnut. Press a ball of filling into each one, close the dough around it, then fashion it into the shape of a crescent.

Place on an oiled baking sheet and cook for 15 minutes. Remove from the oven and dredge each crescent through the confectioners' sugar to coat on all sides.

For date & nut balls, make the filling from 8 oz of date paste or 1¾ cups pitted, chopped dates mixed with ¾ cup each of chopped walnuts and almonds and 1 teaspoon of vanilla extract. Form into balls the size of a hazelnut. Form the dough into balls the size of a walnut, press a ball of filling into each one, close the dough around it, and fashion it back into a ball shape. Cook and dredge with confectioners' sugar, as above.

little "m'hanncha" (moroccan "snakes")

Makes **10**
Preparation time **30 minutes**
Cooking time **15 minutes**

3½ cups blanched **almonds**,
  plus 10 extra to decorate
1½ cups **superfine sugar**
  or **granulated sugar**
⅓ cup **orange-flower water**
1 tablespoon **cinnamon**
1¼ sticks **butter**, melted
10 sheets of **phyllo pastry**
1 beaten **egg**
1⅓ cups **honey**

Chop the almonds in a blender, then add the sugar and 1 tablespoon of the orange-flower water and chop again until fine. Put the mixture in a bowl and add the cinnamon and 4 tablespoons of the butter. Mix to a paste and form into 10 rolls, 6 inches long and 1 inch wide. Set aside.

Preheat the oven to 250°F.

Cut each sheet of phyllo in two. Brush a half sheet with melted butter, top with another half sheet, and brush it with butter. With the long edges facing you, fold over a 1 inch border and stick with the beaten egg. Place an almond roll along the folded edge and roll up in the phyllo, then roll the length into a spiral. Repeat with the remaining pastry sheets and rolls of filling. Place on an oiled baking sheet and brush with melted butter. Press a whole almond into the center of each spiral. Transfer to the oven and cook for 12–15 minutes.

Meanwhile, heat the honey and remaining orange-flower water together.

Dip the cooked cakes, still hot, in the honey mixture and arrange on a serving platter.

For pistachio "snakes," replace the blanched almonds with blanched pistachios and the orange-flower water with rose water. Reduce the quantity of cinnamon to ½ tablespoon and add the finely ground seeds of two cardamom pods. Use a pale, mild honey, such as acacia or clover, for the coating mixture.

gazelle horns

Makes **50**
Preparation time **25 minutes**
Cooking time **15 minutes**

Pastry dough
2⅓ cups **all-purpose flour**
4 tablespoons **butter**, softened
¼ cup **orange-flower water**
2 tablespoons **confectioners'
  sugar**
pinch of **salt**

Filling
3½ cups cups blanched
  almonds
1½ cups **superfine sugar**
  or **granulated sugar**
1 tablespoon **orange-flower
  water**
2 tablespoons **butter**, melted
1 tablespoon **cinnamon**

Rub together the ingredients for the dough. If it seems too dry, add a little water or extra orange-flower water. Let it rest in the refrigerator while you prepare the filling.

Chop the almonds in a blender, then add the sugar and orange-flower water and chop again until fine. Transfer the mixture to a bowl and add the butter and cinnamon. Mix to a dough and form into sticks 3½ inches long.

Preheat the oven to 350°F.

Divide the dough into about 50 small balls. Roll out the balls thinly into rectangles and place a stick of almond paste on each one. Close the dough around the filling, press to seal, and trim to form a horn shape. Place them on an oiled baking sheet.

Transfer to the oven and cook for 15 minutes. Let cool before serving.

For moroccan mint tea to serve six as an accompaniment, bring 8 cups water to a boil. Warm a large teapot with boiling water, then add 3 tablespoons of gunpowder green tea leaves and a little of the measured boiling water. Swish the tea in the water, then strain off the water, leaving the wet tea leaves in the pot. Add the remaining boiling water and let the tea steep for 5 minutes, then add 1 bunch of fresh spearmint leaves and steep for another 5 minutes. Stir in ⅓ cup sugar, then strain the tea and serve garnished with a mint sprig.

pistachio baklavas

Makes **24**
Preparation time **30 minutes**,
  plus resting
Cooking time **20 minutes**

Baklavas

2½ cups raw **pistachio nuts**
½ cup **sugar**
1 tablespoon **orange-flower water**
8 sheets of **phyllo pastry**
1 **egg white**
1 stick **butter**, melted

Glaze

1 cup **honey**
2 tablespoons **orange-flower water**

Dry-roast the nuts in a medium-hot oven for 15 minutes, then rub off the skins and finely chop with the sugar. Add the orange-flower water, then set the mixture aside.

Take 2 phyllo pastry sheets, overlap slightly on the long sides, and stick them together with egg white. Butter generously, then fold in the top and bottom edges to form a rectangle. Place one-quarter of the filling in the center, then fold the pastry sheet over into the center and again to bring in the sides, flattening slightly to make a package around 2 inches wide. Repeat to make a total of four long packages. Place on a baking sheet, cover with plastic wrap, and place a weight on top. Let sit overnight.

Preheat the oven to 300°F.

Unwrap the cakes and place them in a buttered baking pan. Slice each cake into six pieces on the diagonal, using a sharp knife. Do not separate them completely. Transfer the pan to the oven and cook for 20 minutes.

Meanwhile, heat the honey with the orange-flower water for the glaze. As soon as the baklavas are cooked, coat them immediately with the hot glaze. Let sit for 1 hour before removing them from the pan.

For dates stuffed with pistachios, put 1½ cups blanched pistachios in a food processor with ¾ cup confectioners' sugar and 2 tablespoons of orange-flower water and blend to a paste. Make a slit in one side of each date and press in a small pat of paste (this quantity will fill 1 lb fresh dates).

moroccan rice pudding

Serves **6**

Preparation time **5 minutes**

Cooking time **40 minutes**

1 ½ cups **short-grain rce**

1 pat of **butter**

8 cups **milk**

1 cup **superfine sugar**
  or **granulated sugar**

½ teaspoon **salt**

1 tablespoon **orange-flower water**

Cook the rice following the package directions, following the absorption method, using 3 cups of water. Once the water has been completely absorbed, add the butter, milk, sugar, and salt.

Bring back to a boil, stirring from time to time so that the rice does not stick, then add the orange-flower water and continue to stir until the milk has the consistency of a custard.

Remove from the heat and continue to stir to prevent a skin from forming. Serve in a large bowl.

For rice pudding with almond milk, blend ¼ cup chopped blanched almonds in a food processor or blender with ¼ cup of boiling water. Push the mixture through a fine strainer into a bowl, then blend with another ¼ cup of boiling water and strain again. Pour into a liquid measuring cup and make up to 8 cups (2 quarts) with milk. Complete the recipe as above.

honey halva "griwach"

Makes **20**
Preparation time **30 minutes**
Cooking time **15 minutes**

Halva
1 cup **white sesame seeds**
1 envelope (2¼ teaspoons)
    active **dry yeast**
8 cups **all-purpose flour**
4 teaspoons **baking powder**
½ teaspoon **ground turmeric**
pinch of **saffron**
1½ cups of a mixture of melted
    butter and sunflower oil
3 tablespoons **vinegar**
oil, for frying

Glaze
1¾ cups **honey**
⅔ cup **orange-flower water**

Dry-roast the sesame seeds in a skillet over low heat. Remove and let cool.

Mix the yeast in a bowl with a little warm water. Put the flour in a large bowl, make a hollow in the center, and add in all the other ingredients except the oil. Knead the dough thoroughly, then roll out and cut into 4 x 3½ inches rectangles, 1 inch thick. Twist the rectangles and join the two ends.

Heat the oil in a deep-fat fryer or deep skillet and cook the cakes, in batches, until golden on all sides.

Meanwhile, heat the honey with the orange-flower water. Dip the hot halva in the glaze, then sprinkle with the sesame seeds.

For baked halva, beat 1 stick butter with ⅔ cup superfine or granulated sugar, then add 1 cup semolina, 2 teaspoons of baking powder, 1¼ cups ground almonds (almond meal), the finely grated rind and juice of 1 small orange, and 3 extra-large eggs. Beat until smooth. Bake in a greased and lined 9 inch square cake pan in a preheated oven, at 425°F, for 20 minutes, until golden and almost firm. Meanwhile, place 1 cup superfine or granulated sugar, 1 cup water, 1 cinnamon stick broken in half, and strips of rind from 1 orange in a saucepan. Heat gently, stirring, to dissolve the sugar; boil without stirring for 5 minutes. Remove from the heat, discard the cinnamon and orange rind, and stir in the juice of ½ lemon and 2 tablespoons of orange-flower water. Prick the cake all over with a toothpick and drizzle with the syrup. Serve cold.

moroccan pancakes

Makes around **20**

Preparation time **20 minutes**,
  plus resting

Cooking time **20 minutes**

3⅔ cups **bread flour**

1 cup **fine semolina**

½ envelope (1⅛ teaspoons)
  active **dry yeast**

½ teaspoon **salt**

1 cup lukewarm **water**

1 stick **butter**, melted

⅓ cup **peanut oil**

sugar or **honey**, to serve

Mix together all the dry ingredients in a large bowl and add the water little by little, working it in until you have a supple dough. Let rest for 5 minutes.

Divide the dough into pieces the size of a tennis ball and place them on an oiled work surface. Let rest for another 5 minutes.

Melt the butter and mix with the oil. Coat your hands in the mixture and, taking each ball, in turn, stretch the dough into a large, very thin, almost transparent, circle.

Coat your hands again in the butter-and-oil mixture, fold the circles in three, then into three again to form a square, tuck in the ends, and let rest for 10 minutes.

Cook each pancake in a hot skillet for 1 minute, turning over halfway through. Serve hot, with either sugar or honey.

For yeast-free moroccan pancakes, sift 4 cups all-purpose flour into a bowl with a pinch of salt. Gradually add ½–⅔ cup water and, using your hands, work the flour into the liquid until the mixture comes together into a smooth, not sticky, dough. Divide the dough into 20 pieces and roll each into a ball. Complete the recipe as above and serve warm, with honey.

baghrir

Makes **12**
Preparation time **10 minutes**,
  plus resting
Cooking time **12 minutes**

1 ¼ cups **all-purpose flour**
2 ¾ cups fine **semolina**
4 **eggs**
4 cups **milk**
¼ cup **yeast**
½ teaspoon **salt**
honey, to serve

Blend all the ingredients except the honey in a food processor and let rest for 1 hour.

Lightly grease a heavy skillet or crepe pan with a drop of oil and place over medium heat.

Pour a ladleful of batter into the skillet, spread thinly, and let cook for 1 minute without turning. Remove from the heat once the surface of the bghrir is full of holes. Continue to cook the bghrir until all the batter is used.

Serve with honey.

For semolina "soup" with milk & honey, bring 6 cups of water to a boil. Stir in 1 cup of coarse semolina and 1 teaspoon of salt. Gently simmer over low heat, stirring, for about 15 minutes or until the semolina is cooked and the mixture has thickened. Stir in 4 cups milk, 4 tablespoons butter, and 1 ½ teaspoons of ground anise seeds. Bring back to a simmer and cook for another 10 minutes, until thickened. Stir in ¼–⅓ cup of honey, to taste, and serve drizzled with a little extra honey.

fromage blanc with honey

Makes around **12**

Serves **6**

Preparation time **10 minutes**,
plus resting

4 cups **whey**

2 cups whole **milk**

¼ teaspoon **salt**

7 **walnut halves** and
1 tablespoon **honey**,
to serve

Pour the whey into a mixing bowl.

Pour the milk and the salt into a saucepan and bring
to a boil, then pour onto the whey, beating with a hand
whisk. Cover and let rest for 12 hours.

Drain the mixture through a fine cheesecloth placed
in a large colander until the cheese is firm.

Turn the cheese into a serving dish, decorate with the
walnuts, and drizzle with the honey.

For pomegranate seeds with orange-flower water
to serve as an accompaniment, mix the seeds from
6 pomegranates with ¼ cup of sugar and 3 tablespoons
of orange-flower water and stir gently to combine.
Sprinkle with a little ground cinnamon to serve.

index

acknowledgments

Special photography by Michel Reuss.

Other photographs © **Octopus Publishing Group** David Munns 85, 87; Ian Wallace 39, 41, 113, 155, 163, 173; Lis Parsons 49, 95, 97, 109, 151, 153, 177; Sean Myers 77; Stephen Conroy 101, 127; William Lingwood 93; William Reavell 65; William Shaw 115. © **Shutterstock** Philip Lange 2–3; Kippy Lanker 4–5; Eric Gevaert 6–7; Miljan Petrovic 16–17; Bogdan Ionescu 58–59, 186–187; Laurent Renault 70–71; Monkey Business Images 116–117; Nicobatista 140–141; Peter D. 156–157; Hamiza Bakirci 170–171; Farres 196–197; Inacio Pires 232–233.

Executive Editor: Eleanor Maxfield
Managing Editor: Clare Churly
Senior Art Editor: Juliette Norsworthy
Translation, editing, and design: JMS Book LLP
Picture Library Manager: Jennifer Veall
Senior Production Controller: Caroline Alberti